HERDSMEN'S ART
IN HUNGARY

CORVINA PRESS

HUNGARIAN FOLK ART 5

Editor
Prof. GYULA ORTUTAY
member of the Hungarian Academy of Sciences

Herdsmen's Art in Hungary

by JÁNOS MANGA

CONTENTS

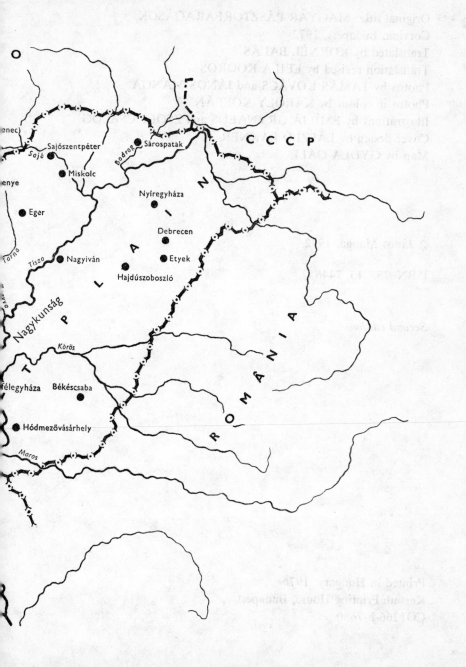

Original title: MAGYAR PÁSZTORFARAGÁSOK
Corvina, Budapest, 1972
Translated by KORNÉL BALÁS
Translation revised by LEILA KOOROS
Photos by TAMÁS KOVÁCS and JÁNOS MANGA
Photos in colour by KÁROLY KOFFÁN
Illustrations by EMÍLIA GRYNAEUS and ZSOLT CSALOG
Cover design by LÁSZLÓ LAKNER
Map by GYULA GÁLL

ISBN 963 13 7446 7

Second edition

Printed in Hungary, 1976
Kossuth Printing House, Budapest
CO1266-h-7680

THE ANTECEDENTS

Art is an expression of the culture of a people and reflects its past, its historical development and socio-economic life. In art particular features may evolve that are common to peoples far removed from one another, and this can be understood in terms of similar ways of life and corresponding historical processes. Equally, neighbouring societies, and even sections within any society, may produce a type of art totally different from each other due to the differing historical developments and traditions. The same conditions also explain why the flowering or decline of folk art, the changing function of decorated objects and the particular styles and motifs of decoration do not always appear simultaneously in neighbouring communities. Thus Gyula Ortutay, the eminent folklorist, writes that historical and social influences varied in the different regions of Hungary and contributed to the emergence of a multitude of regional differences within folk art, also folk music and poetry, and were responsible for its waning and its gradual but final extinction.

Since the way of life and the culture determine the art of a people, any changes in them will affect the artistic activity; the function and importance of objects and utensils will alter and so will the techniques, forms and patterns of ornamentation. It is a fundamental characteristic of folk art that it is never art for art's sake. The decorated objects of folk society are functional articles, tools for everyday living. The way of life, the daily activities and occupations of the people shape the implements in use and they, in turn, express the tastes of the community not only in the form they take, but also in their decoration.

In Hungary, as in other countries, herdsmen formed a distinct group within the peasantry, and their pastoral way of life, tending herds in the solitude of the fields and woods, differed greatly from that of the ordinary peasant. Consequently there emerged what its first Hungarian researcher, Ottó Herman (1835–1914), called "pastoral art". Its roots were in peasant art, but as herdsmen produced utensils to serve their own particular needs which were based on a nomadic existence, and decorated these articles in a distinct style, a separate tradition developed which can be clearly distinguished.

Before speaking of the pastoral life of the Hungarian herdsmen, however, of their decorated utensils, of the techniques and the motifs used, we should examine the common roots. We must make a brief survey of the tradition of decorated objects made for domestic use by the carvers, carpenters and jacks-of-all-trades in the villages for themselves or the peasants, and in the towns by the millers, joiners, coopers, potters, furriers and cloak-makers who belonged to guilds.

While folk art flourished in other parts of Europe, the Turks ravaged Hungary, destroying any Hungarian examples. The oldest remains are from the seventeenth century and, not surprisingly, are found in those regions which escaped the devastation of the Turkish wars. Once life returned to normal, however, everything from houses to the simplest utensils, rebuilt and replaced, fulfilled not just a function but in their decoration they satisfied a craving for beauty.

The earliest surviving examples of wood-carving are on a few cross-

*1 Carved side-gate with rosettes.
Kalotadámos (Damoş, Rumania)*

*2 Carved side-gate with flowers and
the date 1876. Kalotaszeg (Zona Calata,
Rumania)*

*I Back of shaving-mirror frame.
Süttör (Fertőd), Győr-Sopron County, 1866* ▷

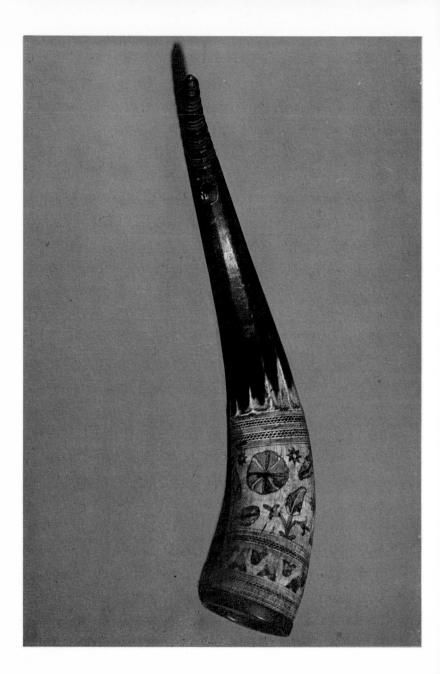

beams, pillars supporting crossbeams, gates and gate-posts. The engraved motif on one crossbeam in Transdanubia—dated 1686—is a rosette. The finest examples of gate-posts decorated with rosettes are to be found in the Kalotaszeg region *(Fig. 1)* and in Székelyland in Eastern Transylvania (today Rumania). The most impressive of ancient carvings, the so-called "Székely gates", are also found in this area. The oldest "Székely gate" known is dated 1673 and its decorative motifs are of a purely geometric nature. It was the gate in the plank fence surrounding the Franciscan monastery of Mikháza.

9

More carved objects have been preserved from the second half of the eighteenth century. A pillar supporting a crossbeam dated 1797 *(Fig. 3)*, a mangling board with the date 1770 *(Fig. 4)* and a razor-case from 1801 *(Fig.5)*. All illustrate the ancient geometric style of decoration, but in addition the rudiments of floral representation appear, although the leaves, the tulip play only a subordinate role in the composition. The design on the mangling board *(Fig. 4)* shows clearly the structural arrangement of the engraved rosettes, stars, rotating wheels, sawteeth and between them the plum-stone shaped leaves.

The geometric decorative patterns of carved wooden implements continue into the nineteenth century. Among their makers we find millers, carpenters,

3 Pillar supporting the crossbeam, 1797

II Drinking-horn.
Borsod-Abaúj-Zemplén County, 1895

coopers, village wood-carvers and herdsmen alike. Geometric patterns, rosettes were applied to distaffs, distaff-soles, grave-posts, hoe-scrapers, spoon-racks, salt-cellars, whip-handles and the hewn linen-chests. Former decorative traditions still survived for some time, and the conventional objects of decoration were detached from usual decorative techniques and patterns only gradually and slowly.

The beginning of the eighteenth century was marked by a decisive change. Although reconstruction of the country started after the devastations of the Turkish wars, the lot of the serfs was still hard during the first decades of that century. They not only had to build their own homes, but they also had to shoulder a major part of building the manor-houses of the landlords, farmsteads, churches, and the many new schools. In the middle and second half of the century, economic boom followed as a result of these steady and uninterrupted efforts. Animal husbandry lost its former importance, agriculture became dominant and there were advances in town handicrafts. Trade developed and as the number of fairs increased, more and more craftsmen worked for villages and the serfs.

Ornamented articles of village or town craftsmen, pottery, painted furniture, embroidered articles of clothing, textiles found their way into peasant houses. Geometric forms no longer appeared as the dominant decoration: instead it was the flower, or the bunch of flowers. The "Italian pitcher", a characteristic pattern of the Renaissance, was known in this country as early as the first half of the seventeenth century. In the first years of the century it appeared on the *Habán* dishes. Later it became the principal motif of book-binding, honey-cake forms, painted ceilings, embroidery, painted furniture and glazed tiles *(Figs. 6 and 7)*. The pomegranate, stylized flowers, flowers springing from a heart and bunches of flowers appeared on all these, filling up the surface to be decorated, at right angles to the base or arranged diagonally *(Figs. 8 and 9)*. Flower motifs came to dominate Székely gates and also wicket-gates, gate-posts and other wood-carvings *(Figs. 2 and 10)*.

Other decorative elements were increasingly applied, in addition to floral designs. Most of the old geometric forms vanished, some of them were occasionally used as border decorations, as if enclosing the central motifs.

Guild signs, religious scenes appeared beside flowers on certain articles of everyday use such as guild-pitchers, guild sign-boards. On others the

4 *Mangling board with incised decoration,
1770. Ferenc Liszt Museum,
Sopron*

5 *An incised razor-case with a
sliding lid, 1801. Museum,
Hódmezővásárhely*

variety of patterns was enriched by pictures and scenes taken from everyday life, from the environment, by animals, and historical and patriotic motifs. Inventive men, engaged in producing beautiful articles, looked for new knowledge, new impressions—so they drew inspiration not only from the familiar things of their environment: the stone carvings of churches, the decorations on furnishings and other pieces in churches and manor-houses, but also from coats of arms on old documents and seals; pictures, illustrations in books; the world of tales and legends, heard or read; historical or other events—all served as sources for their creative work.

The use of more and more decoration on utensils and the general application of the floral ornament are characteristic of popular carving as it continued during the nineteenth century. The peasantry became increasingly interested in artistic objects and the number of peasant carvers decorating articles of their own creation grew, too. The flower took possession of all those spaces which formerly were decorated with rosettes, stars, sawteeth and undulating lines.

The growth of folk art in the nineteenth century was accompanied by the development of a particular style of pastoral carved art closely related to the herdsmen's way of life. Although springing from the common root of all branches of popular art, the herdsmen's craft took a different course in that century. Most of their decorated utensils and implements were integral parts of pastoral life, of herding, and the basic material of the articles was taken from the environment. The decorative technique applied to these articles was many-sided, more varied than that of the peasants. The herdsmen's artistry as a whole, the trends and changes of utensils and their decorations were in close relationship with the trends and changes in pastoral life. Nor can the passing of this art be detached from the vanishing of that ancient way of life.

6 An Italianate jug with a bunch of flowers on a painted wooden ceiling, 1746
7 A stove-tile with flower ornamentation. Székelyland (Transylvania, Rumania)
8 A bunch of flowers growing out of a heart. Painted on furniture. Nógrád County
9 The bouquet motif in transversal arrangement. Panel of a painted wooden ceiling

*10 Gate-post with a chiselled flower
pattern. Komáromszentpéter
(Svätý Peter, Czechoslovakia)*

HERDING—THE HERDSMEN'S LIFE

Transdanubia, the Great Plain and the Uplands, the three regions of Hungary, differ from each other in geography, ethnography and economic history. Since they also differ in animal husbandry, herding and pastoral art, these three areas will be examined separately.

Transdanubia

The Bakony mountain range is a region famous for its pastoral life. As late as the second half of the last century it was described as "...the haunt of the shepherds and swine-herds where the ancient pastoral life of Bakony still survives in its old ways and customs. The persecuted elements of the old society, disrupted by the new ranks and classes,* those escaping impressment, escaped convicts, ruffians, those avengers of the abuses of the landlords, all often sought refuge in the depths of the vast forest after they had been chased away from other regions by the gendarmes of Veszprém or Zala County. Stealing runs in the blood of this crowd of swine-herds and shepherds, too, and they catch the sheep and swine of others to roast at their feast."

There is much truth in this literary description. The herdsmen who came from different places had very often run away from their landlords, or tried to avoid the authorities because of some mischief, theft or ruffianism; they differed altogether from the serf and cotter population of villages in their conduct and way of thinking. The daily life of the latter was determined by the order of manorial power, by the strict and fully enforced economic and moral limits of the village community. The life of the herdsman was one of relative independence, by his standing outside society to a certain degree, by the freedom and the shelter of the forest.

Herding in Transdanubia in the late eighteenth century and first half of the nineteenth, was still nomadic. According to maps from the time of the Emperor Joseph II (1780–90), more than half of Somogy County was forested. A few settlements existed on the edges or in the clearings of these forests, but

---

* A pre-feudal nomadic democracy survived among herdsmen in Hungary until very late, practically the nineteenth century. Feudal organization had a revival from that time.

there were actually no villages within them. Many wayside inns, however, were to be found on the numerous paths that led through the heart of the forests, and these were the meeting-places of the harsh herdsmen, many of them banished from the villages.

At the beginning of the nineteenth century the introduction by the big estates of Merino sheep, or "silk sheep", on a large scale, began to change the unrestrained life of the herdsmen. In one of his treatises written in the early 1820s, Sámuel Kiss wrote: "The underbrush into which it was impossible to penetrate a short time ago and where only the howling of wolves and the unpleasant shriek of moorhens was to be heard, through great expense and hard work has been turned into velvety meadow where the 'silk sheep' graze knee-deep in grass and clover." Complaints about the decline of sheep farming are increasingly heard in the second half of the nineteenth century. To quote a report about Tolna County: "Before the rich grassland was ploughed, sheep farming was pursued by the big tenants, called the 'sheepmasters'; these have gone, and today this 'silk' branch of agriculture is managed by the estates themselves." The drop in the price of wool plunged sheep farming into a critical situation. The big estates changed from sheep-farming to cattle and horse breeding, and only fragments of former sheep farms survived in some places. Following this the sheep population no longer increased and the number of reduced flocks fluctuated in the subsequent decades. This period saw the decline of one-time pastoral life. The old shepherds of the first half of this century still recall those times.

New breeds of sheep did not replace the old ones everywhere at the same time. Some of the big estates changed over to the "silk sheep" only in the second half or at the end of the last century. Consequently the changes in the shepherds' way of life, related to the manner of herding, did not take place everywhere at the same time, nor in the same circumstances. In the memories of the old shepherds who lived at the beginning of this century, the decisive change took place at the time when the German sheep were introduced. During the nomadic days of herding, late in the eighteenth and early in the nineteenth century, the shepherds lived in the forest summer and winter alike. They were sheltered from the rigours of the weather by only a hut or hovel. The life of the shepherd was determined by this permanent stay in the forest and by conditions of life that were primitive

III Swine-herd's horn. Báta, Tolna County, 1898 ▷
IV Gourd. Somogyhárságy, 1933 ▷▷

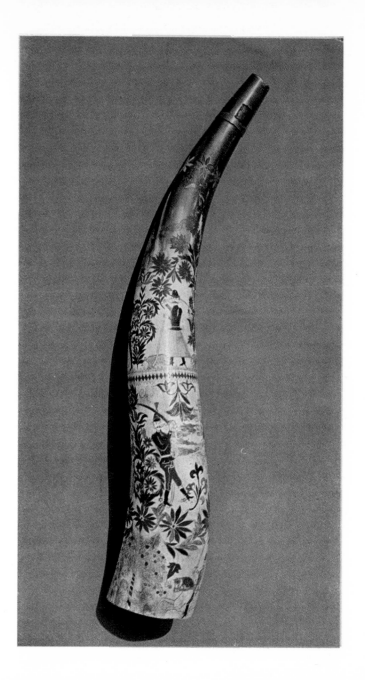

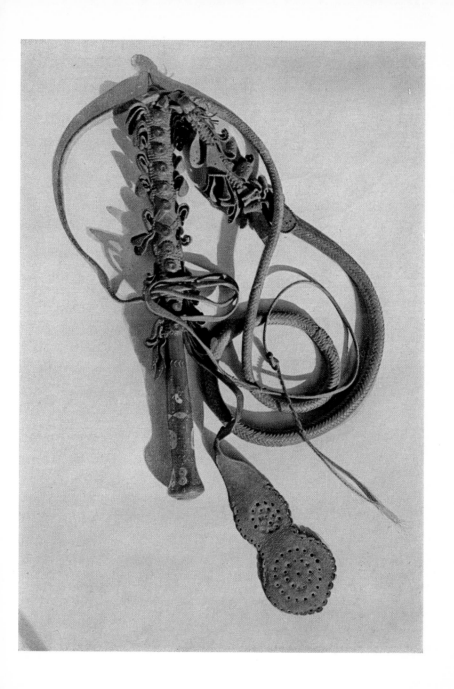

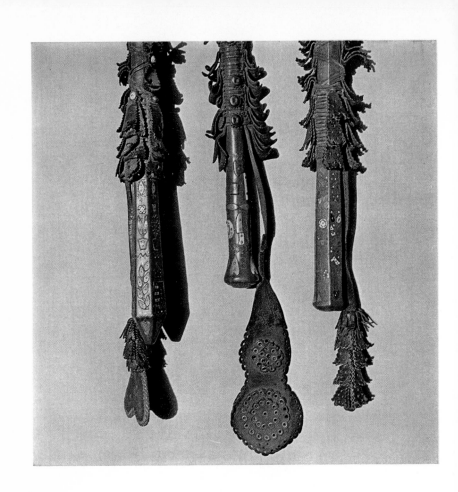

even compared to the standards of the serfs at the time. Houses for shepherds and sheepfolds were not built until after the acclimatization of the Merino. The sedentary job, the constant watch kept over the sheep transformed the shepherd's life considerably: he was now tied more firmly to the landlord, the estate and the village. His financial circumstances, especially those of the head shepherd, improved; but the flocks no longer increased, there was, as we have seen, even a trend towards a decrease. Also the ancient organization of shepherds disintegrated about the end of the last century; the patriarchal relationship that had existed between the head shepherd and the shepherd boys disappeared. The boys were no longer engaged by the head shepherd; they were employed by the landlord who gave them payment in kind. More and more often at the turn of the century

11 Swine-herd from Somogy County, middle of the nineteenth century. After Mihály Szemlér (Historical Gallery of the Hungarian National Museum)

◁ V Horse-herd's whip. Hortobágy
◁ VI Whip-handles decorated with fringed leather-work

old shepherds and their families moved to the village, bought some land there and built houses.

Among the swine-herds those of the Bakony mountains and of Somogy County *(Fig. 11)* were particularly far-famed. In the second half of the last century, Sándor Baksay wrote: "Wearing a heavy mushroom-hat bordered with a broad, black ribbon, the richly trimmed short Veszprém *szűr* (frieze-cloak), a collarless shirt shorter than the middle of his back, short linen pantaloons with numerous long fringes gathered in hundreds of folds, tall moccasins, his black hair parted in the middle, partly falling freely on his neck, partly knotted behind his ears, blustering and swearing— this was the swine-herd. Some of them grew so powerful that what they said went in the brotherhood of swine-herds from Siófok down to Drávafok... And, in the heart of the forest at the camp of the swine-herds, five or six outlaws sit round the fire, sometimes tired, sometimes feasting, and hiding from the county authorities."

The fraternity of the swine-herds was the most notorious of the herdsmen of Bakony. The villages engaged them by streets and this is why they were called street-herders. In olden times they did not marry. From them came most of the tramps, brigands and highwaymen who played such a disreputable role in the history of Bakony. The acorn-bearing woods of Bakony were excellent for pig-keeping. During the eighteenth and most of the nineteenth century, the herds of swine were out in the forests summer and winter, day and night. They fattened on acorns in forest pigsties and were driven from there to the butcher, or home for pig-killing. This variety was called the Bakony pig. In the nineteenth century, however, the curly-bristled Serbian pig was introduced widely, and by the end of that century accounted for 80 per cent of the entire pig population. Replacement of the old variety by another, the resulting transformation in the manner of keeping and the reduction of forest areas obviously affected the herdsmen's way of life.

The decrease in forest areas, planned afforestation and game-preservation forced the herds of swine out to the fields, pastures and ploughlands. These changes, like the former ones, contributed to the transformation of the ancient habits of the swine-herds. The swine-herd now had much more to do with the herd entrusted to his care. He had to drive it home every day and this changed his former free, unrestrained way of life. He was no longer permitted to keep his own pigs and this curtailed his income.

The once fearsome figure of swine-herd was pushed to the bottom of the hierarchy of herdsmen. The children of elderly swine-herds engaged themselves as farm-hands, became day-workers and the swine-herds were replaced by men who did not want to, or were unfit for, doing any other kind of work.

The cattle population of Transdanubia was also considerable. Cattle export to Austria, Vienna had old traditions in this region. Here, too, it was the introduction of new varieties that brought changes. About the situation at the middle of the last century, a contemporary wrote: "Hungarian cattle is raised in herds at several estates—but there are a few Tyrolese and Swiss pens as well... also the common people keep a fine Hungarian breed." Changes in cattle-breeding took place largely about the turn of the century. The number of Hungarian herds had decreased by that time. Although the men tending the herds of cattle also belonged to the community of herdsmen, their job did not always pass from father to son, as did that of the shepherds or swine-herds. The same applies generally to the horse-herds.

We know from the stories of old herdsmen that the shepherds and the swine-herds were the most famous among them. In the last century, these occupations were usually handed down from father to son. It was not until the turn of the century that the son of a swine-herd turned cowherd, shepherd, or vice versa. Nor was it rare later on for a herdsman to hire himself out now as a shepherd, now as a swine-herd, now as a cowherd.

The community of herdsmen had its own rules to govern personal contacts, address, beliefs, customs, dress as well as, naturally, the tending and curing of animals. This was also the case in the other regions of the country. Shepherds cultivated contacts, friendship and family relations with shepherds, swine-herds with swine-herds, because intermarriage was common among them. Now and again they visited one another, invited one another to saints' days, weddings, christening feasts or funerals. When they gathered in the fields of a village, they passed time in the nearest inn. In some herdsmen communities it was customary to visit a place of pilgrimage once every year. They turned up at church twice a year at best: at Christmas and Easter.

The customary address between the head shepherd and between the common shepherds was "brother-in-law", but the head shepherd called his men and boys by their first names, while they addressed him "Sir" or "my elder brother".* The head shepherd ranked first in this hierarchy; he was followed by the senior shepherd, then by the shepherd boys. The boys had to take orders from the head shepherd and the senior shepherd alike.

The usual subjects of conversation among shepherds, swine-herds and cowherds whenever they met on their daily range were herding, highwaymen or outlaws, and they compared their carved articles. Older people would pass on knowledge to the young about the birds and animals of the forest, about trees and plants and the natural environment in general, and instruct them in tending and curing their animals. True and legendary stories about the feats of herdsmen and highwaymen of the past were also related on such occasions.

Yet behind this apparent strictness of social conventions there was a great diversity in individual attitudes and conduct, and in the level of education.

Although herdsmen of the past were usually illiterate, some were not and they carried books, almanacs, trashy novels or prayer-books to read while the herd grazed. There were men among them who were driven by the desire for knowledge, while others were interested in nothing but the herd and nature. Some knew all about trees, others knew the names of all field and forest plants and flowers. The names and feats of famous herdsmen and highwaymen were known to most of them. A few of them had a sprinkling of historical knowledge. From the cleric's point of view herdsmen were not religious people, although as we have seen, some of them were familiar with the legend of a saint or a passage from the Bible and visited places of pilgrimage regularly. Some were satisfied, others were of a wild disposition. They considered it a crime to harm the poor, but not to cheat the squire, to steal or to disobey the authorities. Vengeance was fairly common among them.

Their beliefs, their rituals differed from those of the peasantry in many a respect. Herdsmen too, knew and had heard of witches, incubuses, ghosts, but they concerned themselves with these much less than the peasants.

* As a peculiarity of the Hungarian terms for family relations, elder brother and younger brother are denoted with distinct words.

Herdsmen were noticeably less superstitious than the peasants. At the same time peasants believed that herdsmen, especially swine-herds, had the power to make sick or cure swine with magical practices. Naturally enough, the beliefs of herdsmen were interwoven with the bewitchment and healing of animals and with the magic properties of certain plants and animals such as frogs and snakes. Like the peasants the herdsmen celebrated the occasions of birth, marriage and death and the holidays of Christmas and Easter. Because the families of the herdsmen lived in isolation, however, they did not belong to communities preserving homogeneous traditions, and their observances were neither as uniform in practice nor as important as those of the village or region.

The Great Plain

Great similarities existed between the herding practices of the Plain regions and those of Transdanubia. The differences were produced mainly by changes that took place in the relationship of agriculture and animal husbandry, and also by the chronological differences of these changes. The first striking difference is that many elements of the herding tradition survived on the Great Plain into the twentieth century. These traditions preserved the different varieties and transitional forms of nomadic and semi-nomadic animal keeping. Environment deeply affected the methods of herding and the herdsmen's way of life. In this area were to be found dry, unwooded flat-lands, shrubby swamps and reedy patches rich in vegetation. The distances between human settlements were immense. Given this harder existence, the demands for clothing and implements were not so exacting in standard as in Transdanubia.

The *Kiskunság* district, lying between the Danube and Tisza rivers south of Budapest, is a typical herding region of the Great Plain. A mere hundred years ago pastoral life flourished everywhere. Horses and cattle grazed on undivided pastures.

Flocks of sheep were driven on the fringes by shepherds and herds of swine entrusted to swine-herds grubbed about in boggy places. The transformation of nomadic animal keeping, where the herd and the herds-men lived in the open, winter and summer alike, began early in the last century. It was followed by semi-nomadic farming differing from the former only in that the stock wintered near farmsteads, in sheltered places. Where no such space was available, nomadic stock-farming continued.

Some years ago an 80-year-old shepherd told us that about 1900 sheep were still kept in the open, through the entire year, in the fields surrounding Kiskunfélegyháza. When the snow had fallen, wheat-straw was carried to the sheep; they fed on it, and what was left was used as bedding. The accumulated bedding was then used for surrounding their quarters. In one corner of this fence was the shack, made of reeds or straw, in which the shepherds sheltered. Big pens were constructed for the stock on big estates. These pens usually had three sides made of adobe, and a roof covered with straw.

The traditional way of shepherding in the Kiskunság district was gradually abandoned in the second half of the last century when consolidation of the land strips began. Driven out of the common pastures farmers sold most of their stock and most of the pasture was ploughed up. In areas where the pastures were left intact, shepherding continued, though on a reduced scale.

Old herdsmen of the *Hortobágy*, this most famous herding region of the Plain, can still recall how winters were spent on the *puszta*. In olden times when the stock wintered there in the open even in the coldest weather, the spots best for wintering, hollows protected by tall reeds, were selected well in advance. In an area large enough to accommodate the animals, reeds were rolled down. A path of flattened reeds served as an entrance and exit for the animals. Standing tall reeds protected them from the wind and snow-storms while those underfoot combined with manure to preserve the heat below. The herdsmen also took shelter here in circular shacks made of reeds whose walls were smeared over with mud or cattle manure. Where no such shacks could be erected, the men slept under the stars enveloped in their sheepskin cloaks *(suba)*.

Bálint Tóth, a 72-year-old shepherd of Hajdúszoboszló, told us that when he was young they used to go out with the flock in spring and only returned home in winter. When they drove out the sheep, they arranged the sheep-pen and lodged there as long as the weather was cool and rainy. Later on, when the weather turned warm, they packed their belongings, food and vessels for cooking, on the donkey and moved along. Wherever night overtook them, they stopped, unloaded food from the donkey, prepared their meal and lay down to sleep. Their frieze-cloak *(szűr)* or sheepskin cloak served as bed, blanket and pillow. When autumn set in, they returned to the place from which they had set out in spring. The first snow had fallen by the time they started homewards with their flock. **23** It was no rare occurrence to start in mid-December and only get home on New Year's Day.

The most famous herdsmen of Hortobágy were the horse-herds. Even at the close of the last century the horses of some big estates wintered in the open. The open-air wintering place was a large pen encircled by a high fence made of horizontal wooden bars. Such pens were also erected for cattle. There was always a thick layer of manure in the pens to preserve warmth. Grazing and caring for the stock were adjusted to the requirements of agriculture. Colts under three years were not driven out until the snow had thawed. One head horse-herd together with his hands was sometimes in charge of as many as six or seven hundred horses. Once the agricultural spring-work was done, the draught-horses were driven out, too. Farmers usually kept one pair at home to do the daily chores. When the harvesting was over, all the draught-horses were driven home to help in gathering in the crop. Mares producing good foals were kept in the open pasture from spring to autumn. Mares and their foals were driven home in November.

In the early years of the nineteenth century various forms of animal husbandry and herding adjusted to developing agricultural production and differing according to land and region, emerged everywhere. These changes involved certain restrictions of free animal keeping, grazing and the imposition of rules on herdsmen. As early as 1755, the horses of the herdsmen were taken away at Kiskunhalas, although they were still permitted to keep horses and a cart for themselves at Dévaványa in the middle of the last century. There it was part of the herdsmen's allowance to keep two horses and three cows. But the keeping of horses was prohibited also here after some time; branding of the animals was made obligatory, and in accounting for a dead animal the complete hide had to be handed over, not only the ears as before.

Although there were numerous herdsmen in the Great Plain whose ancestors had pursued this trade for generations, their moving to other regions was much more frequent in the nineteenth and twentieth centuries than in Transdanubia. At Kiskunfélegyháza, about the turn of the century, many families of herdsmen existed whose ancestors had lived here, but many families had moved there from the Hortobágy. Shepherds, cattle-herds and horse-herds used to move from Kiskunfélegyháza to the Hortobágy. The horse-dealers, who wandered all over the regions of the Great Plain, brought news of where herdsmen were needed. Herdsmen from Heves, Borsod, Szabolcs, Gömör, Zemplén and Szatmár Counties used to show up in the last century in the Hortobágy region every year when jobs were being bargained.

There were differences between the herdsmen of the Great Plain and those of Transdanubia in their beliefs and religion. Some herdsmen of Hortobágy, in the second half of the last century, did not allow their men to work on Sundays or holidays except for keeping watch over the flock. Curing sick animals was also forbidden on such days, and it was not permitted to eat until everybody had said their prayers. Swearing, however, was characteristic of most of them and those who thought themselves religious were probably more superstitious than God-fearing. One of them told us his father was twenty-five when he attended church for the first time, and when the organ began to play, he started to whistle for "it played such a beautiful tune".

They believed that certain people possessed the evil eye and such people were not attacked like strangers by dogs. They were afraid of spotted dogs and black cats because they were held to be creatures of ill omen. It was forbidden to beat a dog to death, because the cattle would have perished as a result. Nor was it permitted to hang or beat a cat to death, because a member of the family would have died in this case. Most of the herdsmen at the turn of the century still believed in witches. They were convinced that both men and animals could be bewitched and whenever some disease broke out in the herd, they attributed it to the evil practice of another herdsman. When a shepherd was angered by another, he revenged himself by threading a needle with the hair of a scabious sheep and sticking it into the skin of one of his enemy's sheep. As a result the whole flock became scabbed. All these attitudes, this world of beliefs have gone; they survive only in the memory of old herdsmen, and soon even these memories will be preserved only in written records.

What we call the Uplands is the hilly and mountainous region lying north of the Great Plain and comprising Nógrád County, most of Heves and **25** Borsod-Abaúj-Zemplén Counties, as well as the northern parts of Pest County. In the hilly regions of the Uplands the most important branch of animal husbandry in the nineteenth century was sheep-breeding. Before the introduction of the Merino the ancient Hungarian variety was kept. Although the improved varieties appeared in Hungary as early as the first half of the nineteenth century, they became widespread only in the last decades. A report on Nógrád County, dated 1847, says that "there is not much to be said about cattle and horse-breeding; sheep farming is more important, and the wool market in Losonc [Lučenec] shows that this branch is developing in both quantity and quality. Sheep are kept also in the northern mountains, but only the variety with coarse wool..." Božena Němcová, a Czech authoress, who visited Nógrád County on two occasions in the early 1850s, wrote that "two varieties of sheep are bred in this region. A Hungarian breed called 'Racka' which have coarse wool and are used to make fur-coats, sheepskin cloaks and sleeveless woollen cloaks *(guba)*; only as many Racka as are necessary for these are raised. The second breed, 'Merino', has very fine wool and these are bred in great quantities."

In the fifties of the last century, the hills and mountains, the clearings in wooded areas of Nógrád and Heves Counties abounded in sheep-pens and shepherds' houses built by the estates or by shepherds tending their own flock. Grazing was usually in the vicinity of the pens, and lasted from early spring until the hard winter had set in. The barren sheep were driven out in spring when the snow had thawed, about St. Joseph's Day—March 21—the ewes and the lambs at the end of March or in early April. In other places all sheep were driven to the pasture on March 19, because it was held that from this day the flock could subsist in the fields. The flock grazed in the fields from morning till night, but when the lambs had been weaned, the ewes were driven home at noon and milked. Although the abolition of common pastures in 1880 and the drop in the price of wool reduced the number of sheep, there was an upswing again at the turn of the century. For instance, as many as 20 or 30 thousand sheep were driven to the Losonc Fair. Some of the big estates in this region kept

10–12 thousand sheep. Sheep farming amongst the peasantry varied from village to village. Peasant farmers in villages along the Ipoly river sometimes kept 30–40 sheep, sometimes even more.

The shepherd's task was twofold: he had to protect and tend the flock, and had to avoid harm during grazing. Packs of wolves frequented the wooded hilly regions and the Great Plain in the last century and if the shepherd was not alert they decimated the flock. A greater danger, however, were the brigands, who sometimes drove away complete flocks. The shepherd's person was also endangered in such cases, and his most important defensive weapon was his ax which he kept on him even when he was asleep. The ax served other purposes as well; when a sheep's leg got caught in the roots of a tree, or its horns in the branches, the shepherd cut it free with his ax. Since flock was often pastured close to cultivated areas, the shepherd had to watch that the sheep did not damage the green crops or vegetables, because he was held responsible for any such damage.

According to old practice, an estate or farm only engaged the head shepherd, and it was his responsibility to hire men. In the hierarchy of shepherds, it was the head shepherd who had real authority. Head shepherds of large estates that kept numerous flocks were not engaged in ordinary guarding work, they only supervised their men. It was therefore that an order of rank was established among the head shepherds: at the top was the head shepherd who supervised the common shepherds, and at the bottom was the village shepherd who looked after the sheep of the farmers of a given community. As in Transdanubia shepherds thought themselves superior not only to other herdsmen, but to the peasants as well. The story goes that when a shepherd and a peasant were engaged in litigation, the judge told the shepherd at the hearing: "Márton, you should come to terms with the farmer." The shepherd replied: "Me, with a peasant?" "Why," asked the judge, "what are you after all?" "Me, I am a shepherd", was the answer.

The acorn-bearing forests of the Uplands yielded food not only for sheep, but also for swine. Pigs, fattened on acorns in the Upland regions, yielded a considerable income to landlord and serf alike. One manuscript from the early years of the eighteenth century says of the forests of Cserhát: "In these vast virgin forests extending in some places for five miles, Austrian oak *(cser)* grows in abundance everywhere (this is where the name of the region comes from). Gigantic trees grow here and Nature offers these acorn-covered grazing grounds to the swine with such generosity that the population of the region can make their living for a year through them. The barrows fattened on acorns are driven in herds to the mining towns of the region, and all of them are sold there. There are quite a number of peasants who live with their squire's permission in the depths of the forest."

The reduction of wooded areas, giving up the practice of foraging for acorns, brought changes to the ways of pig keeping and changed the life of swine-herds. The poorest grazing grounds were left to the swine, and the swine-herd had to live in the open from morning till night, summer and winter, in rain or snow. Here, too, he was pushed to the bottom of the herdsmen's hierarchy. But it was this very swine-herd whom popular belief endowed with mysterious talents and capacities. Only a few decades ago, older swine-herds at the Ipoly river still had the reputation of being witches and were thought capable of bewitching or curing humans and beasts alike. A few of them were adept at love magic and knew remedies for winning back faithless spouses. It was amongst the swine-herds that the bagpipers emerged whose instruments in popular belief sounded even if they were not blown. We know from the stories of old men that sorcerer swine-herds were able to do miraculous things.

Old people living at the Ipoly told us that there was once a swine-herd in a village who used to play his bagpipe for the young men during the three days of the carnival celebration. On Shrove Tuesday, when the "bagpipe dance" was over, and the men were drinking in the inn, the village swine-herd—the bagpiper of the dance—entertained the lads with various stories about witches. When the lads doubted his magic powers, the swine-herd pulled the sleeve of his frieze-cloak, shouted "Shoo! Out!" whereupon nine piglets jumped out of the sleeve. The piglets ran about on the table for a while, then the swine-herd shouted "Shoo! In!" and the piglets disappeared up the sleeve of the coat.

DECORATED BELONGINGS
OF THE HERDSMEN

At the end of the eighteenth and the early years of the nineteenth century, the Hungarian herdsmen society, even if the landlords sometimes engaged herdsmen of foreign origin, mainly comprised old families and preserved the ancient pastoral traditions. As we have seen in the preceding chapters, they essentially differed from the peasantry not only in occupation and ways of life, but also in their attitudes. Herdsmen were conditioned differently by their free life remote from the peasant communities, by solitude, the nearness of nature, the hardships of life in forests, fields and the endless plains, by rains, snow, storm and cold, or by the scorching heat of the sun. Their desires and ambitions were driven in different directions. They had to produce most of their belongings and implements themselves and they took the models from other herdsmen, or were motivated by things they had seen elsewhere which they considered useful for their work. That varied and rich set of implements which the Hungarian herdsmen created in this way does credit to both their inventiveness and sense of beauty.

The use of implements and the manner of their production passed from father to son in herdsmen communities, too. In the course of everyday work, driving, pasturing and tending the flock, the younger generation learned all that their ancestors knew.

Although the implements made by the herdsman-artist were needed by all, they were produced and decorated only by those who were fond of carving. The inclination to carve unfolded in the young boys under the influence of older men engaged in carving. Good carvers never forgot where, when and with whom they had seen the first decorated article that had struck their fancy and inspired them to carve. Many of them often spoke of their masters who had instructed them in all the ins and outs of carving, and taught their pupils how to select the material for the implement to be produced, and how to compose the designs. We know of young herdsmen who acquired their skill in carving merely through silent observation, and after many attempts were able to produce several articles. There were others who developed into well-known carvers of a neighbourhood by getting practical advice from older herdsmen.

In addition to inclination and ability something else was required: the herdsman-artist needed a good pasture, a peaceful noonday rest to find time for carving. Watching the flock did not always take up all his time, not even on poorer grazing grounds. He could always find some leisure time, and carving was never work—it was pleasure, distraction and a pastime. Success, the creation of a fine piece, praise, and the interest shown by others encouraged him. Some of them saw the purpose of their artistic work not in the production of some useful thing—but rather in the pleasure derived from the process of creation. Most of these men copied all the pieces and utensils that had been made by their masters, their ideals, but we also found among them some who specialized in carving and decorating only certain objects. The choice of objects and patterns for carving was also determined by the materials available in their environment. It is not by chance that an abundance of wooden utensils is found in the various regions of Transdanubia which are rich in wood suitable for carving. The salt-cellars and drinking-horns made of horn, on the other hand, were common everywhere because material was provided by the horns of slaughtered or perished cattle.

The Implements of Driving and Tending

The herdsman's most important driving implement, and his favourite belonging at the same time, is still the *stick*, shaped to fit his purposes and to meet his taste. It was, and still is, used by swine-herds, shepherds, cowherds or horse-herds of the Great Plain, the Uplands and Transdanubia alike. One end is usually thicker than the other, and the thicker end usually has a butt *(Figs. 12 and 13, Plates 20 and VII)*. This stick served a variety of purposes in the hands of the one-time herdsman. He leaned on it during his watch, threw it at the animals, sat on it, and killed small field animals with it.

12 Shepherd's stick with tin inlay

It also played a role in the pastoral dances, and was the herdsman's weapon in case of need. The sticks were of different lengths. In 1800 the local council of Kiskunhalas prohibited the carrying of long knobsticks. There is contemporary evidence that the shepherds used to carry sticks six feet long with them. Because this region was poor in wood suitable for sticks, sticks made of cornel-wood were taken from as far as the Bakony mountains to the fairs of the Kiskunság. But thornwood, wild pear, sorb, oak, and—in the Great Plain—occasionally even willow were also used. The bark was steamed over a fire, then stripped off; the stick was then placed in manure to become red, and finally rubbed with tallow or fat *(Plate 9)*.

During the last century sticks with tin inlay at the thicker end were used by the herdsmen all over the country *(Fig. 12, Plate 20)*. The tin inlay decorated the stick, and made it heavier so that it was easier to hit a target with it. In some regions of Hungary, the thickness and form of the stick indicated to whom it belonged. In the Hortobágy region, the cowherds had the thickest sticks with knots and the biggest knob; the sticks of the horse-herds were thinner, and the thinnest of all were used by the swine-herds. The latter even bent their sticks lest they should injure the pigs when hitting them. Sticks decorated with copper plate, inlaid with metal, horn, bone, or caoutchouc were widely used, especially by the horse-herds in the Hajdúság region, and at the Tisza and Körös rivers after the turn of the century *(Fig. 13)*; it was fairly general practice to put a ring at the thicker end of the stick. This ring, made of the shank-bone of cattle, or of horn, was about 5–6 cm. wide.

In Borsod County the copper-plated sticks were called *horse-herds' sticks*, but pretentious shepherds, swine-herds and cowherds also had such sticks for festive occasions. Thirty to forty years ago the price of such a stick was a weaned piglet. In the neighbourhood of Sárospatak, the swine-herds and cowherds used the *headed stick* or the *button-headed stick*. Herdsmen used simpler ones on their watch but they took decorated sticks when they went to a feast, visited friends or went to the fair. In Nógrád, Heves and Borsod Counties, as in wooded regions generally, *knotted sticks* were much in favour. The branch of a wild pear or sorb chosen for the stick was gashed with a knife in spring, or punched with an awl; by autumn interesting calluses and knots developed on the branch. This knotted branch was then cut off and steamed in its bark; after removing the bark, the stick was covered with lime, or was placed in lye, then rubbed with fat or tallow to give it a pleasant red tone.

The richest collections of sticks are to be found in the museums of Transdanubia. The most interesting of these are sticks with handles carved like human heads, human and animal figures. Such sticks were made not just by people who usually did woodwork. One stick in the Museum of Székesfehérvár, with a lizard on its handle, is said to have been carved by Mór Jókai, the famous novelist, for Nándor Zichy as a token of remembrance of the time they spent together in prison after the War of Independence. The herdsmen called these sticks "walking-sticks", and carved them usually

13 A flattened out design taken from a shepherd's stick with inlaid horn and bone. Made by Gyula Kádár in Dévaványa in 1928

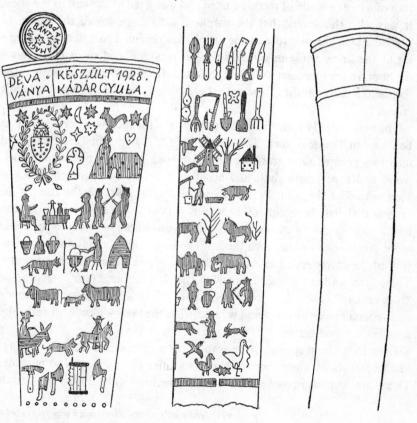

as a present for somebody. Beginning at the end of the last century, sticks decorated with raised woodwork and having a bent handle, called the *crooked sticks*, became increasingly popular. They were much in demand in Transdanubia during the years following the turn of the century and were carried by cotters, forest rangers and peasants alike. Carver-herdsmen made a gift of these to the farm-bailiffs, overseers, relatives or friends whom they regarded worthy of it. To others they gave them in exchange for wheat, lambs or piglets. Old herdsmen, who were no longer employed, carved sticks for sale.

One type of stick, which was usually called *shepherd's crook*, was only used, and is still used in many places, by the shepherds. When necessary, they caught the sheep with this stick. The crook proper was cut from the root of a tree or made of metal or horn and was fixed to the end of the stick. It was with this crook that the shepherd caught the leg of the sheep. In Transdanubia the aperture of the crook was designed to catch the sheep's leg at the knee, while in other regions it was designed to catch it above the hoof. In the representations of the first half of the nineteenth century, the shepherd is distinguished from other herdsmen in that he holds a shepherd's crook.

The most varied forms and finest specimens of the shepherd's crook were to be found in Transdanubia *(Plates 7, 8, 10, 11, 12)* and they can be divided into two groups. One group contained crooks made of pieces of cornel-wood and sorb where shaft and crook were made of a branch that had been cut off at the root. Part of these, in conformity with the root of the branch that had been cut off, represented now a human figure, a human head, now a ram, a ram's head, and so on. Others—and this is found more often—had crooks with the head rounded off where the short extension of the crook ended in a ram's head, a dragon's head, a rose or acorn. These were called in accordance with the decorations "ram", "acorn" or "rose crooks". The other group consists of sticks where the crook is made of a separate piece of wood and is fastened to the shaft—usually of sorb—by a nail or a wood-screw.

Even today, a shepherd, if he wants to be considered worth anything, has several sticks, since shepherds' crooks differ also in respect to purpose. There are *watching-crooks* used by the shepherd only during his watch

VII Herdsmen's sticks. Hortobágy and Dévaványa ▷
VIII Swine-herd's ax. Őrhalom, Nógrád County, 1911 ▷

over the flock, and there are *gala crooks* carried when going to town, or visiting, or going to fairs *(Plate 11)*. Needless to say, the watching-crook is the simpler one, the gala crook is more decorative. Shepherds sometimes distinguish the head shepherd's crook from the boy's crook. According to the recollections of some shepherds, the shaft of the *head shepherd's staff* was thin, that of the *boy's stick* was thicker. The crook proper of the gala stick was often carved of ram's horn, shaped as required after softening in hot water. Shepherds also use crooks of iron or copper; these were usually made to order by blacksmiths.

The driving tool of the swine-herd, horse-herd and cowherd is a *long whip*. It is made up of two parts: the whip-lash, always made of leather for a herdsman of any standing, and the handle, which is usually short, the length of the forearm, and is decorated as a rule *(Plates 6 and VI)*. Herdsmen preferred handles made of the wood of the plum-tree. Animals respect the long whip more than any stick. This is not so much for beating as for cracking and driving the herd with shouts. The horse-herds of Hortobágy, galloping on horseback, lean forward and drive the horses rather by cracking their whips than hitting with it. When a storm breaks, the horses tend to bolt, especially if there is lightning; the horse-herds encircle them, making great, cracking noises with their whips, and shout to keep the horses together.

Herdsmen of artistic disposition have always been fond of making whips; they carved the handle and braided the lash themselves *(Plate V)*. Sometimes, too, one herdsman braided the lash from strips of leather and another carved the handle. Handles were decorated in a number of ways: besides carving, old whip-handles are often decorated with tin inlay, metal plating and metal inlay. Decorations were applied to the upper half of the handle, but on recent specimens from the Great Plain this part is covered by braided leather and the inlaid decoration is on the part that serves for grasping the handle.

The implement for tending the animals, and the herdsman's weapon, was the ax. The ax-head was made by blacksmiths, the helve by the herdsman. It was mostly swine-herds that still used the ax in the last century *(Plate VIII)*. When a pig's leg was jammed in the roots of a tree, the herdsman freed it with his ax; it was with his ax that he cut the branch best

◁ *IX Mirror-case with sealing-waxed decoration. Around 1840*
◁ *X Mirror-case with sealing-waxed decoration. 1856*

suited for making a stick, that he defended himself against a raging boar, against the wild boar, wolves and snakes. There were still quite a number of swine-herds in the middle of the last century who were highly skilled in handling the ax: from a distance of 20–25 yards they were able to give the pig a blow behind its ear with such a force that it collapsed at once. When they performed the swine-herds' dance, they struck at one another with their axes, producing sparks when the heads clashed together. Then they hurled them into the ceiling joist. The authorities kept prohibiting its use, because this dangerous tool was used whenever there was a fight.

In 1791 Veszprém County issued strict orders for confiscation of axes for herdsmen. In 1822 the carrying of an ax was prohibited for the following reasons: "...whereas the axes usually carried by cowherds, common shepherds and swine-herds ordinarily only serve the purpose of being employed by evil-doers for endangering the life of other men of good will and for disturbing public safety, such herdsmen shall henceforth not be permitted to carry their axes on them when following their herd."

This is what Ottó Herman wrote about the notorious ax of Somogy County: "The swine-herds of Somogy in particular are immensely proud of this weapon, keeping and concealing it in defiance of all prohibitions. The helves of finer specimens are polished and almost entirely covered with the most various products of the swine-herds' decorative imagination, such as human and animal figures, and there are real masterpieces among these ax-helves. The culmination of this ornamentation was a mirror the size of a silver florin inset in the helves of axes made for famous highwaymen and swine-herds. The highwayman ran his mirrored ax into the earth, took out his multi-coloured razor-case, picked the tricky lock, and shaved under the sky."

The *swine-herd's horn* was made of the horn of Hungarian-bred cattle. Sometimes they were as long as 80 centimetres. Some of them were made even longer by attaching a metal piece to the lower end. The top, where it was blown, contained a simple hole, or was shaped into a mouthpiece similar to that of the bugle. Some swine-herds fixed a brass mouthpiece— the one used with bugles—to the top end. The swine-herd blew his horn for some seconds at various intervals as he drove along the street the swine swarming out of the yards. The swine-herd's horn also made its way into folk customs. In many places the swine-herds used to wander through the streets on Christmas Eve, or New Year's Eve, blowing their horns and cracking their whips, and the pig-owner farmers gave them presents at this time. According to the 1649 Charter of Incorporation of the herdsmen of Vas County, the herdsmen had to attend the procession on Corpus Christi

Thursday, then partake of the sacrament. "When all this is done, all of them must go righteously to the Guild-master"—the Charter went on—"and must blow their horn once in front of the Guild-master's house..."

Although the horns used by swine-herds as a rule had no decoration on them (the initials of the user were carved in some of them), skilled herdsmen made decorated horns. Our museums keep decorated pipes from the upper reaches of the Tisza river, from Gömör County (Czechoslovakia), Nógrád County and Transdanubia; but we have no information on whether the swine-herds actually used them. These were probably made as decorative pieces for the swine-herds, or for others—for sale—or served as hunting-horns for forest-rangers, foresters or huntsmen. Pál Gyurkó, a swine-herd of Nógrád County, made a finely decorated pipe in 1899, but did not use it. It was placed in a museum. Antal Kapoli, the outstanding artisan-shepherd of Transdanubia, made many horns with engraved decorations and always called these "hunting-horns" *(Plates 33 and 34)*. The finest specimens of horns inlaid with Spanish (sealing) wax are kept in the Museum of Szekszárd *(Plate III)*.

The Utensils of the Herdsman

The horns of dead cattle were used by the carvers for a variety of purposes, not only for the making of horns. Everyday articles were made of them for which wood was not suitable, or more correctly, for which horn was better. Tools and utensils made of horn or bone have a fine tradition. Historically and practically it is the *drinking-horn* that stands foremost of objects made of horn *(Plate II)*.

Some types were known and used all over the country. The *drinking-horn* in the Museum of Debrecen bears the date 1819 *(Fig. 14)*. In all probability, this piece is a later copy of the original made in 1819. The drinking-horn dated 1851 and kept in the Museum of Győr is of similar execution, but is longer and its decoration is different.

The drinking-horns we have mentioned above were actually sawn-off sections of cattle horn, shaped into drinking-vessels by applying a bottom to them. In the recollections of aged herdsmen, drinking-cups made of horn were also used in Hont, Nógrád and Gömör Counties; they were carried in satchels, or fixed to the satchel strap, or in the sleeve of the frieze-cloak. These cups were 10 to 14 cm. tall, and the thicker end of the Hungarian cattle's horn was taken to make them. Their bottom often consisted of a wooden plug, or a horn plate, or a metal plate. Some made a groove at the thinner end of the sawn-off horn, softened the groove in hot water, and inserted a circular horn plate, also softened beforehand, into the groove.

The drinking-vessels made of horn are simpler, evidently also older; the type widely used in the past is known to us from the territory east of the Tisza river *(Plate II)*. This type of vessel, called "drinking-horn", was actually one piece of the pointed end of cattle-horn, which was sawn off about 25–40 centimetres from the point. This vessel was still in wide use in the second half of the last century—we know of pieces bearing different dates from that period—but by the turn of the century only a few aged herdsmen used it. Its use is described by István Ecsedi: "If the land round him was marshy, the herdsman always carried his drinking-vessel on him; this cow's horn was tied by a long leather strap to the rosette of the frieze-cloak strap, hanging downwards and placed under the felt cloak to protect it from the heat of the sun; for if it warmed up, the water had an unpleasant taste. When such a herdsman pressed down on the saline bank, the water rose and he scooped it up and drank it."

14 Drinking-horn with scratched and incised pattern, 1819

The herdsmen of Békés County hold that the ox-horn was used for drinking at the time when there was water everywhere, that is before the swamps and the dead-waters had been drained. As late as the turn of the century, the swine-herds in the neighbourhood of Sárospatak still used the drinking-horn—especially in winter—when buckets were removed from the wells in the fields. The swine-herds fastened the whip to a ring at the wider end of the drinking-horn which they then lowered into a well to scoop up water. The sharp end of the horn was cut off lest it damage the sleeve of the frieze-cloak or the satchel, and also that it should occupy less room.

The pointed end of the drinking-horns belonging to the other type was left intact; a hole was sometimes made in that end, and the horn was fastened through this hole to the rosette of the frieze-cloak strap. A hole was often bored in the flared end of the horn, and leather fringes were threaded in this. Besides such fringes, these drinking-horns were decorated: the pointed end, where their colour was black, was often cut in a multi-angular fashion and decorated with notched, raised rings. To the end where the black colour of horn turns white, they applied similarly raised, notched decorations. While the former type—with the point cut off—must be regarded in every case as drinking-horns that actually were used, most of the latter were made as decorative pieces.

After the drainage of the swamps and the drilling of wells, drinking-horns became unnecessary and were converted into salt-cellars and whet-stone holders. In the Museum of Nyíregyháza one can see a drinking-horn which has been transformed into a container for a whetstone used to sharpen scythes.

Herdsmen used to carry their salt on them—together with food—as a matter of course. The best material for *salt-cellars* was horn, because it protected salt from water and moisture. Salt-cellars made of horn were common in all corners of the country, and were used not only by herdsmen, but also by peasants, forest rangers or hunters. Some of the specimens in the Museum of Kiskunhalas warrant the conclusion that the salt-cellars and scab-grease cases of this region were cut from the thinner end of the horn to a length of some 10–12 centimetres. The lower, wider part of this piece was sealed with a circular wooden plug; a hole was bored in the top end, and also sealed with a wooden plug. The salt-cellars of Kiskunfélegy-háza, which the shepherds kept in the sleeve of their frieze-cloak, were of this type. The herdsmen of Dévaványa often carried two such cellars: in one they kept salt, in the other they kept paprika.

At Hortobágy, and along the upper reaches of the Tisza river, a different form was used: sawn off from the middle of the horn to a length of about 12–16 centimetres, one end slightly tapering. The bottom and top openings were sealed with wooden plugs. The box was filled with salt through one of the openings, and a small aperture made in one of the plugs served for salting. This aperture was closed by a small wooden plug, or with a sliding wooden or metal plate. The third type, too, was made from the middle of a horn; it differed from the former in that it was shorter, and that before the bottom and the top lid were cut to shape, the horn was softened in hot water, and pulled on a wooden mould of oval shape to make the salt-cellar not cylindrical but flatter—a more convenient shape to keep in the pocket or satchel. Some of them had a lid, held by a hinge or a snap fastener.

These three types illustrate the trends and changes in the forms of salt-cellars *(Fig. 15)*. The oldest is certainly the salt-horn of Kiskunság, whose one variant is the salt-cellar dated 1814 and kept in the Museum of Debrecen. The second type is the cylindrical salt-cellar made of the middle section of the horn, and the third type is the oval form. That the salt-cellars of cylindrical form preceded the oval ones is evidenced also by Transdanubian specimens. In Transdanubia, where the oval salt-cellars were in general use in the second half of the last century, a few herdsmen still produced cylindrical ones at that time.

15 Various types of salt-cellars and scab-grease cases
from the Great Plain and the Uplands

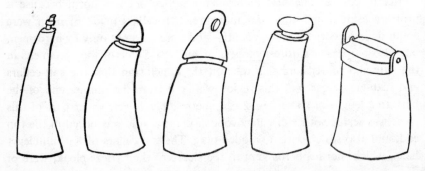

The herdsmen of Somogy County knew two types of salt-cellar: the one was called a "satchel salt-cellar", the other a "camping salt-cellar". The first was small, the second much bigger. These two types were named after two kinds of herdsmen. The satchel-herdsman was the one who drove his herd home every day, and carried food on him for one day only; thus his salt-cellar was smaller and was kept in his satchel. The camper-herdsman stayed in the fields day and night, and kept his food, salt-cellar, shaving-mirror, razor-case, etc. in his shack or hut. His salt-cellar was larger, and sometimes more decorated. Here, too, the commonest techniques of horn decoration were scratching and chiselling; these two sometimes appear together when the very thin lines scratched with the knife's point widen into grooves. On Transdanubian salt-cellars this scratching and chiselling technique is enriched with colourful sealing-wax inlays, consisting of floral ornamentation and scenes taken from the life of herdsmen and high-waymen *(Plates 24–26)*.

At the time when herdsmen still cured the animals entrusted to them, their indispensable remedy was scab-grease, or the scab ointment with which they treated scabies; so was copper vitriol for diseases of the hoof. The devices for carrying these were similar in shape to that of the salt-cellar *(Plate 36)*. A hinge and a snap fastener were applied to the lid by the blacksmith, so that the case could be kept locked and the grease did not flow out. A metal ring was sometimes provided on the lid, and this was fastened to the herdsman's belt by means of a leather strap. Old herdsmen

used to carry the scab-grease case, the sheath of a knife and a tinder-box on their belt. The scab-grease cases went out of use when modern medicaments were introduced.

Both salt-cellars and scab-grease cases were related in material and form to *gunpowder flasks*, and also to the *snuff-cases* that were so much in vogue in the eighteenth and nineteenth centuries. Gunpowder flasks with scratched decoration and yellowed by nitric acid were modelled on salt-cellars and scab-grease cases, and the forms of oval salt-holders were applied to making snuff-boxes.

In Transdanubia, about the turn of the century when herdsmen began to carry pocket watches, *watch-chains* made of horn and bone appeared to imitate metal chains *(Plate 32)*. The ornamental parts of the chain were carved of white or black horn or bone; the links of the chain were always made of horn. The chain-links were cut of horn that had been softened in hot water; the loop was then cut through, bent out, and coupled with the part made of bone, or with the next link, after which it was bent back. When the chain-links made of horn cooled and stiffened, they retained their original shape and did not come unhooked. Similar to the metal chains fashionable about the turn of the century, these chains of horn were sometimes made with several strings. Various pendants were carved of cattlebone or stag-horn. The colour effect of horn-chains was often enhanced by alternating links of darker or black horn with those of white bone or horn.

In hilly and mountainous regions rich in woods, such as Transdanubia, in Northern Hungary, Pest, Nógrád, Heves and Borsod Counties, small *water dippers* cut of wood were increasingly used from the middle of the last century, and gradually supplanted the vessels made of horn *(Plates 37–40)*. In no other country did such a variety of forms and decorations of this vessel emerge as in these regions. In this vessel the herdsmen preserved a utensil which in the past was the travelling companion of wanderers and hunters alike, and which was carried fastened to the belt or to the strap of the satchel. Starting with the sixteenth century this vessel has been represented in genre paintings and conversation pieces.

The water dipper, commonly called *csanak*, was used by shepherds, swine-herds, cowherds and horse-herds alike, especially in areas where springs were frequent. Like their predecessors, the herdsmen usually car-

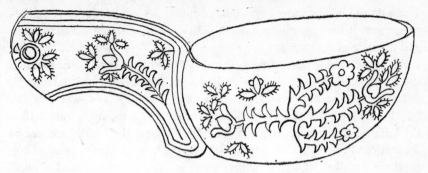

16 Water dipper with chiselled decoration, dated 1841. Museum of Miskolc

ried it fastened to the strap of the satchel, or in the satchel. Because it was exposed to sunshine and wind, the water dipper was cut of dry wood that was less likely to crack, preferably the wood of the plum-tree, wild pear, thorn-bush, maple or linden-tree. For cutting it the herdsman needed a curved knife in addition to his carving-knife; he used the former for shaping the cavity of the vessel. The rich varieties can be divided into two forms: those shaped like a spoon, and those shaped like a cup. Each of them has a cavity for scooping water, a handle or an ear. Variety is characteristic of both shape and handles. Apart from the multitude of variants found in Northern Hungary or Transdanubia, there exists a form which is only known in Transdanubia, particularly in southern Transdanubia. This is the "bowl-form" *(szilke)* whose close relatives occur also southwards beyond our national frontier; it is characterized by chiselled geometric motifs, with occasional inlays of sealing-wax.

In the 1930s some herdsmen in Borsod and Heves Counties still practised the profession of making such water dippers. Old István Mészáros of Sajószentpéter made them to order for herdsmen, hunters and forest rangers. The handle of a dipper made for a cowherd was decorated with a bull's head; the shepherd's dipper had a ram's head, the swine-herd's vessel a pig's head. The decoration of vessels made for hunters and forest rangers was the oak-leaf and the acorn. The cowherds gave an autumn goat, the shepherds a lamb, the swine-herds a piglet 5–6 weeks old. Hunters paid in money.

Five or six carver-herdsmen were known in Heves County in the 1930s.

These decorated the water dippers with raised flowers, oak leaves, acorns, pigs, rams, herdsmen, hunters, and the like. They often carved their name and the date of making. József Ostoróczki *(Plate 4)*, a swine-herd of Egercsehi, began cutting water dippers in the 1920s. In the beginning he imitated the forms of shepherds' spoons he had seen. These were called "round". After some time he chose another form, called the "long sort", or the "duck-bill-spoon". The forms called "round cups" were more varied than the long type, in respect to both the overall shape, the handle and raised decorations. Two types of these are the most frequent: one where the cup proper is rounded off, and the other which employs different forms of cups. We think it probable that the spoon-shape was more frequent in the past. One such decorated specimen, dated 1841, is kept in the Museum of Miskolc *(Fig. 16)*.

The most striking feature of all these water dippers is the great variety of the handles: these mostly represent stylized animals, such as the snake, dog or pig. A swine-herd said: "Sometimes we imitated those of others, sometimes we wanted to make something else, something different. I kept quite a lot of designs. There were designs with dogs, with the deer, stag, wild boar. I copied the designs from the spoons of others. I invented designs myself, of course. Once I saw a heraldic lion on a shop catalogue and copied it as a design right away."

Among the tools for tending the sheep were the *lamb-marks*, also called *lamb-trainers*, or *lamb signs*. These small wooden objects such as boots, violins, axes, pistols, laundry beaters, flasks, spoons, forks, were made in pairs, and the bigger was suspended on the neck of the ewe, the smaller on the neck of the lamb. In this way they knew which lamb belonged to which ewe. Although the making of these cannot be regarded as art, the variety of forms certainly reveal the herdsman's inventiveness and his observation of the environment.

Up to the turn of the century, and even later, the *mirror-case* was among the most important utensils of the Transdanubian herdsman. It was made of wood, and was square, or oblong, or circular, or heart-shaped in rare cases; it consisted of a base and a lid, and contained a mirror inside *(Plates 29, 42; IX, X, XII)*. The mirror was protected from damage and breakage by the lid, which was attached in different ways. That of the square or oblong boxes was slipped into a slanted groove cut in the base. The lids of circular cases had small bolts which fitted into the openings in the base. These mirror-cases were the forerunners of the pocket mirrors of our days; they were in great demand in the middle of the last century when twirled moustaches and the use of moustache-pomade became fashionable among herdsmen. When Milfajt, the notorious outlaw of Transdanubia, had his portrait drawn before his execution at Veszprém in 1836, he looked at it and said that he had had much finer ones beneath a small mirror, and that those had been the portraits of Marci Zöld, Becskereki and Palatinszki (who were hanged in Heves County in 1816) but that he had lost them when he was ill. We assume that Milfajt referred to a mirror-case on which the portraits of those men were painted.

The mirror-cases produced in Transdanubia in the forties of the last century were square as a rule, and their decorative technique was sealing-wax inlay work. Similar square or circular mirror-frames were worn suspended on the girdles of Bosnian women about the turn of the century. Most of the mirror-cases of Transdanubia have a small hollow at the base in which the moustache-pomade was kept. Varied forms and decorative techniques appeared in the second half of the last century: there was scratching in addition to sealing-wax inlay and relief carving was used at the close of the century.

Transdanubian herdsmen usually mention two sorts of mirror-cases, the *pocket mirror-case* and the *satchel mirror-case*. The bigger ones, which would not go into the vest pocket, were called satchel mirror-cases, and so were those which had a hinged lid that could be propped up. The latter were used mainly for shaving. The wood for both types was selected according to the requirements of decoration. For mirror-cases to be decorated with wax inlays and scratching, white wood was used.

Besides pocket and satchel mirror-cases the Transdanubian herdsmen produced prop-up mirror frames which they kept in their shack or at home. The base of these often contained a small drawer for the razor, soap and brush *(Plates 16,XI)*. About the middle of the last century these shaving-mirrors were decorated with scratching and sealing-wax inlay, and relief carving appeared about the turn of the century *(Plate 15)*. At the close of the last, and in the early years of this century, decorated frames were carved for letters of discharge, devotional pictures and photographs.

In the Nagykunság and Hortobágy regions, the *mirror-frame* or *mirror-*

case was much in favour with the herdsmen of the last century. The Museum of Debrecen keeps several specimens of these; there are forms rounded off at the two ends with inlaid tin floral ornaments, semicircular forms reminiscent of the Romanesque style with etched and yellowed decoration, as well as book-shaped pieces with engraved lines and flowers. The semi-

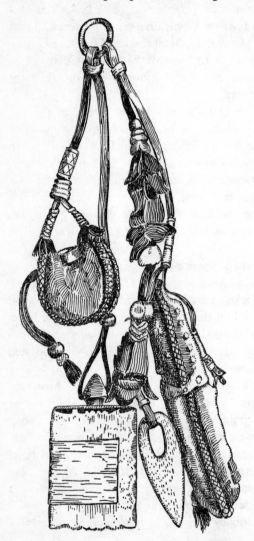

17 *A herdsman's outfit with steel, flint and tinderbox, knife-sheath and mirror-case. Nagykunság region, Great Plain*

circular specimens are dated 1842, 1843, 1850 and 1864. One of the book-shaped mirror-frames bears the date 1850. We assume that these various mirror-cases were used by the urban and rural population alike in the last century. Some of these pieces seem to have been made and decorated by skilled craftsmen.

It was the herdsmen of Hortobágy and Kiskunság who preserved the set of implements called the *herdsman's outfit*. It is made up of the mirror-case, or mirror-frame, the jack-knife sheath made of leather, the pouch for holding the flint and tinder, and a piece of steel used to strike fire, suspended on a leather sling *(Fig. 17)*. All these tools hung on leather straps, threaded into a brass ring, and adorned with metal or bone rings and fringes; by means of the brass ring the herdsman fastened the entire set to his leather belt. Some herdsmen fastened it to the clasp of the frieze-cloak so that they hung into the sleeve of the cloak. At the time when the herdsmen were still wearing moccasins, this set of utensils also contained a bone tool shaped like a small dagger which was used for widening the holes of the moccasin. Some herdsmen carried their round-headed wooden spoon by tucking it beside the knife-sheath.

Ottó Herman aptly remarks that this complete outfit, sometimes called the "pouch", the equivalent of the gentleman's dressing-case, was the herdsman's greatest ornament upon which he lavished all his ideals of beauty. With this set of tools and utensils our herdsmen preserved the equipment and the practice of the wanderers, drovers of the sixteenth-eighteenth centuries because they, too, carried their necessary effects in a similar manner, suspended on their belts. Such sets were known and used then in Hungary, too, which is proved by a piece of steel and part of a purse found in the archives of the town of Cegléd. Tradition has it that this tool, dating back to 1723, was the official charge of the town magistrate. When the fire in a house went out, and the family had nothing with which to relight it, the magistrate's duty is said to have been to kindle a light for them again with his set of steel and flint.

What has remained in use of these sets is only the holder of the *jack-knife* (a leather sheath). The use of the complete sets was gradually abandoned in the second half of the last century. Antal Balázs, a herdsman of Hortobágy, discharged from the army in 1883 where he had got used to matches, no longer used the old fire-striking set, and the steel vanished from his outfit. The pouch was still carried for a while as an ornament but disappeared eventually, and only the sheath of the knife was retained.

Travellers used to carry their *gourd* hanging on the belt or stick *(Plate 35)*. The use of this vessel dates back to the remote past, and it has always served to keep drink in. Its great advantages were that it could easily be made at home from a gourd, that it kept the water cool, and that it was not as fragile as crockery or glass. In Hungary this vessel was used by town-dwellers, villagers and herdsmen alike; they kept water, wine or brandy in it. The poet Ferenc Faludi (1704–1779) has put into verse a riddle about it:

> *Fable, fable, what is this: Has no legs and goes about?*
> *Fable, fable, what is this: Has no soles and stand about?*
> *If you guess right, you may have my gourd,*
> *Or, if you like, my Légrád knife for good.*

When Transdanubian herdsmen grazed their herd in fields where there were no springs and wells, they took water with them in the bottle-gourd. Some old herdsmen still used it after the turn of the century, fastening it with a leather strap to their satchel. They grew these gourds themselves. The seed was planted in spring, and the fruit ripened by October. After plucking the gourd they suspended it in the chimney for several weeks— sometimes several months—to give it a fine red colour in the smoke, and to prevent damage from wood-worm. A hole was then bored—or burned with a hot wire—in the stem, and the seeds were removed by shaking. A rod was put into the gourd and whirled to clean the dried pulp from it, after which water was poured in to separate the residual pulp from the shell. The gourd treated in this way was then decorated with fine incising, scratching, or—less often—with sealing-wax inlays. The decorations incised or scratched as fine lines were sometimes coloured a darker yellow by using hydrochloric acid. Finally a wooden plug was cut for sealing it. We know of people who produced and decorated bottle-gourds as an occupation, and sold them at fairs. In the 1920s and 30s a few herdsmen still made bottle-gourds, but only as ornamental pieces for buyers *(Plate IV)*.

With the invention and spread of the phosphorous match match-boxes carved in bone—or more rarely in ivory—for use in the towns made their appearance. Such match-boxes were needed because of the highly inflammable nature of the matches. For instance, if a herdsman stretched himself out on the matches, which before were kept in a thin box, they were likely to catch fire when their heads rubbed against one another. The Transdanubian herdsmen made *match-boxes* cut of wood—mainly of maple-wood, wild pear or plum—or sometimes of bone and horn. A piece of wood, corresponding to the length of the matches, was hollowed out; the lower aperture was sealed with a piece of wood, and an opening lid was cut for the top. The lid was retained in the open position by a piece of wood, acting like the spring of a pocket-knife. When the lid was closed, it gave a sharp click from the pressure of the wooden spring *(Fig. 18)*.

There were match-boxes with lids opening at both ends. Both sides of the box, or only one, were notched by carving, or a piece of sand-paper was glued on them for easier striking. These match-boxes were decorated with scratching, sealing-wax inlay and relief work *(Plates 27, 28 and 30)*. Match-boxes of similar construction were occasionally made by herdsmen in other regions of the country. At the turn of the century, János Barna of Nógrád County made match-boxes of cattle-bone and stag-horn, and decorated

18 The design of a Transdanubian match-box

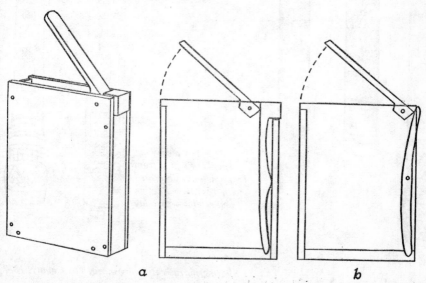

a   *b*

19 Transdanubian
shepherd's flutes
with scratched design

20 A two-piece long
shepherd's flute from
Transdanubia, decorated
with a scratched design
and sealing-wax inlay

XI Shaving-mirror case. Jánosháza, Vas County, 1877 ▷

them with religious scenes. The more frequent form, however, was a small box the length of the matches and provided with a sliding lid; some of these were decorated, but the majority were not. When the phosphorus matches were superseded by safety matches, the match-boxes that had existed only a few decades gradually disappeared from the herdsmen's outfit.

Some herdsmen were fond of singing and instrumental music. They produced their own instruments—some of which they decorated. The most popular and widely used instrument was the shepherd's flute or pipe; specimens with the most beautiful decorations are known from Transdanubia *(Fig. 19)*. Two types were common here: the *flute* and the *long flute (Fig. 20)*. The length of the former varied from 35 to 40 centimetres, or was even longer in some cases; the latter was nearly one metre long, and as a rule, both were made of elder. They were sounded by blowing air through the opening of a wooden plug. The flute had six stops, the long flute had five. In other parts of the country various types of the shorter, six-stop flute were used; the *cross flute*, mostly incised with geometric decoration, was known in Transdanubia and elsewhere.

A much-favoured instrument, used widely in every region of Hungary during the last century, was the *bagpipe*. Bagpiping continued to be very popular in some parts of the country at the turn of the century. This instrument was preserved longest by the herdsmen, who were its real masters. Herdsmen of an artistic bent also decorated the wooden parts of this instrument. The bagpipe-head was shaped sometimes as a goat's or ram's head, sometimes as a human head. Upland herdsmen decorated their goat-headed bagpipes with copper plating, or with mirrors set in a heart-shaped copper frame. The appendage of the chanter was decorated with a carved lute or foal, the stem of the bourdon with raised rings and inlaid tin. The preferred material for the wooden parts of the bagpipe was the wood of the plum-tree.

The *zither*, also called *tambura*, was a popular instrument of the herdsmen of the Great Plain. Although there were occasional incised decorations on the sounding box or the side of some of them, the artistic skill of the makers was manifest, first of all, in the shaping of horse-heads for the lowland tamburas. These horse-heads were carved on the planks of the tambura on which the tuning pins are fastened.

XII Upper and lower leaf of a mirror-case. Nemespátró, Somogy County

We should like to mention in brief the *knives* and *pocket-knives* which the herdsmen made for their own use. The commonest among these were the knives whose blade was reset from a worn-out razor or scythe, and the haft was cut of wood or stag-horn. Mainly to prevent splitting, the haft was decorated with tin ferrule before the blade was driven in *(Plate 5)*. The popular tool of the herdsmen of Transdanubia was the pocket-knife which they called *kusztora*. The haft was made of wood or horn; a brass ring, often prepared from a cartridge hull by filing, was applied to the top of the haft where the blade was fixed. This ring protected the haft from splitting; a nail for fastening the blade was driven in through this ring, and the top flange of the ring supported the blade when it was snapped open. The blade was made from the pointed end of a scythe in most cases. The oldest such specimen dates back to the early years of the last century. The hafts of these knives were decorated. We often see hafts whose lower end is shaped as a boot. Hafts of this form were also made by cutlers. The technique of decoration was scratching, incising, sealing-way inlay, and relief work. Tin inlay was used occasionally. The wood of the spindle-tree was used for making hafts in most cases because scratched or wax-inlaid decorations showed up very well against its light colour. After the turn of the century, when herdsmen went to town and fairs more often, the pocket-knives of their own make were replaced by mass-produced articles.

Carving for Others

Certain implements, both plain and decorated, were not part of pastoral life since the herdsmen carved for sale or as gifts. These were often made for relatives and friends as presents, or by order for fellow-herdsmen, strangers, and villagers. It was fairly common practice after the Great War to produce such articles for sale, or for museums and collectors. A few old herdsmen carved decorated pieces as an occupation, and many a fine specimen was taken abroad.

First there was the *razor-case*, of which various forms and specimens decorated with different techniques are to be found in Hungarian public collections *(Fig. 5; Plates 13, 14; XIV and XV)*. This wooden case reflected the inventiveness, sense of form and good taste of the herdsmen engaged in carving. It served to hold and protect the razor. They were to be found in the homes of herdsmen, peasants and townsfolk alike, and similar pieces were produced by peasant carvers, artisans, forest rangers wood-working to pass time, and even the inmates of prison all made razor holders—and so it becomes difficult to tell their exact origins. Yet it proves that there was interaction in the shaping and decoration of articles produced by herdsmen and others, and that the rich variants of form, decorative technique and patterns emerged as a result of such interaction. The principal types of razor-cases may be grouped as follows:

(a) with one longitudinally sliding lid; some of these could be hung on the wall;

(b) book-shaped cases, with one or two lids sliding longitudinally or laterally on the top or the back or both;

(c) cases with turning lids of one piece;

(d) cases with turning lids of two or more pieces.

Amongst the razor-cases in museums the ones with sliding lids are probably the oldest, although the other types were already being made at their time. In the museums of the Great Plain we see two different forms of the cases with longitudinally sliding lids: one is prismatic, the other has one or two semicircular ends. The prismatic ones were used all over Hungary, and their use spread—quite naturally—also beyond the frontiers. The oldest specimen known, dated 1768, is from Transdanubia; others are dated 1792 and 1799. The lid of the first bears an engraved tulip; two cocks are seen between two roughly chiselled tulips on the other; the third shows semicircular lines bordered with chiselled sawteeth, with the sun in the centre of an arc. The razor-case with chiselled decoration dated 1801 and kept in the Museum of Hódmezővásárhely belongs to this group.

21 A razor-case from the Kaposvár Museum with a stylized floral design in sealing-wax, 1813

The book-shaped forms are extremely varied, and according to the notes about the museum specimens, they come mostly from the Great Plain. At the turn of the century Ecsedi noted that they served to accommodate the soap and the brush, and had the form of a broad book. He said that the herdsman cut cases to the form of the familiar psalm-book or the Bible; their principal decoration is the Hungarian Crown, or a rosemary planted in a pot. Sometimes the rather scanty decoration consists only of quite unsystematic geometric patterns and the date. Chip-carved decorations of geometric character appear on the oldest specimens; floral ornamentation is employed on more recent pieces. Among them are finely worked specimens with etched and sealing-wax inlaid floral decoration, with coats of arms, inscriptions, figurative representations, but the makers of these were not herdsmen, they were artisans in possession of the skills and special tools of their trade.

Razor-cases with turning lids were known to Hungarian herdsmen, and produced by them as early as the beginning of the last century. From the 1810s on, cases with black and red sealing-wax inlays were frequent in Transdanubia. The lid of a razor-case, marked 1813 and kept in the Museum of Kaposvár, shows a stylized flower *(Fig. 21)*; representations of the human form appear later on, in addition to geometric border decorations and stylized flowers *(Plate 13)*. Razor-cases with turning lids of a later period have sealing-wax inlaid decorations; scratched decorations are also frequent, but relief work became dominant on razor-cases by the end of

22 A Transdanubian razor-case. The design incised in on one side shows a hunter's burial

the century. Diversified decorating techniques and decorative patterns were followed by a variety of forms about the middle of the century. Cases prepared to accommodate two razors were frequent, and so were the various clever solutions for locking lids made up of several parts. About the end
of the century, and during subsequent decades, various figures appeared on the lids—the human figure, birds, snakes—amid relief carvings, and the one-time utensil gradually became ornamental only.

A group of razor-cases with turning lids exists which were produced in prisons. This is often made clear by the inscriptions they bear, like the one on a razor-case of the Museum of Pécs: "This razor-case belongs to Mártony Pósa, it was made in the prison of Pécs by János Hollósi, on October 6, 1852." Several Transdanubian museums keep razor-cases on which the "Hunter's burial" is incised and, often, coloured *(Fig. 22)*. Two of these were made in the jail of Sopron in 1872. The inscription on one razor-case in the Museum of Miskolc reads: "Made for József Molnár in Remembrance of His Imprisonment, 1884." It is a known fact that in the first half of the last century, and later, many Hungarian herdsmen were sent to prison where in many cases they served long terms. It seems probable that a considerable number of these inscribed razor-cases were made by such imprisoned herdsmen although the social status is never noted in the inscriptions. The style of the razor-cases made in the prisons of Pécs and Sopron indicates this beyond any doubt.

The next implement, often made and decorated by herdsmen, was the

mangling board. Naturally, it was not a utensil belonging solely to the pastoral way of life; for mangling, smoothening out and glossing the linen after laundering, was done by the families of herdsmen, peasants and townspeople alike. To meet urban needs it was produced by the artisans of the town, while herdsmen and peasants made their own. Decorated mangling boards were made to order, or as a present. They were often given as wedding presents. Slovak herdsmen used to give mangling boards to housewives as a Christmas gift. The oldest mangling boards in Transdanubian museums come from the second half of the eighteenth century; accordingly, their characteristic is the incised, geometric decoration, but occasionally leaf-work and flowers also appear amid rosettes, stars, etc. *(Plates 17* and *18)*. Traces of red paint or sealing-wax are often found in the incised lines and grooves. From the twenties and thirties of the last century, the geometric patterns were gradually replaced by flowers, by representations of the human form, and by religious and patriotic motifs which were also coloured in sealing-wax. The mangling boards, however, did not survive the emergence and general application of woodwork in relief because hemp linen as a dress material was replaced by fine linen.

The carving of *wooden spoons* was a typically pastoral task in Hungary as elsewhere. The oldest forms were the undecorated spoons with a round bowl; decorations were applied only to the handle of the later types which imitated the shape of oval metal spoons. Old herdsmen used wooden spoons a few decades ago saying that they preferred them because they did not burn their mouths since they did not conduct the heat from the hot food. Herdsmen used to carve *wooden forks* with decorated handles. Both spoons and forks often have a short chain at the tip of the handle, carved out of the same material as the handle; pendants shaped as acorns, padlocks, and the like hung on these chains. Before wooden spoons and forks were replaced by metal ones, an indispensable fixture in both peasant and shepherd's homes was the *spoon rack* hanging on the wall. Although such racks were sold at fairs, herdsmen made their own for domestic use. The talent of the carver-herdsmen was obvious in the shaping of the head and handle of the stirring shovel, the peculiar tool of cooking in the kettle over the open fire. Another utensil made by the herdsmen of the Great Plain was the *kettle-ring* or the *dog's spine*. Around Kiskunfélegyháza, it was made of small pieces of willow about one inch thick fitted together, and it was placed underneath the kettle to prevent it from tipping over during the meal.

As recently as the turn of the century, herdsmen of Heves and Nógrád Counties carved *salt and paprika-cellars* out of wood, decorated with relief carvings and modelled after the ones produced by glass-works. Some of them decorated the handle of the salt and pepper-cellars with cocks, birds, dogs, foxes, and attached a pair of lids that could be turned around a bolt fixed in the handle. They made cubic, prismatic and cylindrical salt-holders that were hung on the wall; their decoration was the incised rosette as a rule. They also made match-boxes to be hung on the wall, and all these were fixed on the wall out of the reach of children. *Spice-boxes* were made in Transdanubia, with sealing-wax inlay decorations similar to those on mirror-cases. Decorated *distaffs* occur in both the Uplands and Transdanubia; in the latter region they were made of hazel or spindle-tree and decorated with scratching. The same woods were used to make *pipe-stems* and the frames of spinning wheels.

The *frames* were decorated with inlaid sealing-wax and later on with relief carvings, especially in southern Transdanubia. The *shuttle,* which forms part of a loom, is a small boat-shaped device, by which the weft is passed through the web during weaving, and these in southern Transdanubia were usually carved out of maple-wood and decorated with inlaid sealing-wax. *Laundry-beaters* with incised decorations occurred fairly often. This multitude of decorated utensils and implements was produced mainly by Transdanubian herdsmen. Among these—especially about the turn of the century and the subsequent decades—were many *sockets for antlers, cigarette-cases, tobacco-boxes, cigarette-holders*, various small boxes, as well as *chairs* and *towel-racks* usually with relief carvings.

In the second half of the last century, open-work ornamentation on the *backs of benches and chairs, clothes-racks* became popular in Nógrád County. Old herdsmen recall that these were carved mainly by shepherds for their own use, or for others to order. The pieces of open-work decoration were made individually, first sawn out, then carved, and finally inserted in their places. The motifs had an extraordinary wide range Open-work benches were often called "*hussar benches*" because the back—just like clothes-racks or the back of chairs—was populated with hussars galloping with sabres drawn, modelled on the hussars seen on honey-cakes, or on the letters of discharge *(Plate 31)*. There was hardly a herdsman's house without an ornamental bench with an elbow-rest. These pieces of furniture were also fashionable in peasant homes.

The decorated back panels of these benches were made of beech or oak. The hewn pieces of wood were roughly smoothed first with an ax or adze, then with a plane. The patterns to be cut out were then drawn on the boards with a pencil. Holes were bored at certain points of the drawing, and the contours of the decorations were sawn out with a whip-saw. After sawing, the patterns were refined, improved with a sharp knife, and eventually smoothed down with sand-paper. The carved panels were then fitted into the frame of the back of the bench-chair or of the clothes-rack, which had been prepared beforehand. On the back of the bench made in 1900 by Mihály Bertók, a former herdsman of Kishartyán, the following decorations were made by sawing: oak-tree, hussar, stag, sheep, herdsmen with pigs or sheep, bagpiper, dancer, and so on. Pál Lőrincz of Karancskeszi, a former shepherd, told us that "everybody carved patterns to the best of his abilities. Animals, oak-trees, birds in the trees, squirrels... Shepherds and bagpipers having a good time under the trees... the Hungarian Crown was also there". He added that he did not carve hussars, because he did not feel like it. The backs of some benches had houses, trains, or religious scenes. Mihály Bertók told us: "I had a bench that was more showy than the midnight Mass."

Ornaments, Small Sculpture, Carved Pictures

It appears from the listing in the foregoing that the carver-herdsmen preserved their old traditions, familiar objects, decorative techniques and patterns for almost a century and a half. Their artistry did not become stereotyped, but adjusted to the changing needs of everyday life. Utensils and tools that had become unnecessary died out, and new needs created new articles. The increase of carved utensils continued through the turn of the century, but many of these gradually lost their close relationship with pastoral life. Old familiar items were still produced, but ornamental work became their dominant feature. Some lost their original function, and the artist-herdsman produced them no longer for himself or fellow-herdsmen, but for the interested public, for collectors and museums. The number of

XIII Water dipper, Nógrád County, 1898 ▷

carvers who were herdsmen by profession decreased at the same time, and more and more people, having abandoned the pastoral way of life, did woodwork out of habit, as a hobby or to make some money. The traditions of decoration survived, but became disengaged from the ways of life that produced them and in which they had flourished.

We have observed this process since the turn of the century, especially in the decades following the First World War. Of the more recent objects we mention the walking-sticks of diversified forms and decorations, the horns and other articles made by Antal Kapoli senior and junior, various boxes, cigarette-boxes having the form of a salt-cellar, and the like. In Nógrád County one can see how the carved panels in the backs of benches were transformed into hangings for the wall, containing partly the old figures, partly imitations of devotional pictures. Ram's heads, sockets for antlers, clothes-racks carved of wood and hanging on the wall became fashionable in Transdanubia after the turn of the century.

The most popular form of fine work of some herdsmen was "The Suffering of Christ" placed in a bottle. This complicated creation was in great demand among peasants about the close of the last century, mainly through the herdsmen who found time to produce it. János Berze, a carver-herdsman of Heves County, sold one such piece for two pengős in the 1930s. As he put it, "to assemble the sufferings of Christ in a bottle was a suffering in itself". The crucifix, the instruments of torture, the coffin, the cock and the pigeons comprised thirty-six carved pieces and they were put together in the bottle by means of long tools made from knitting needles and parts of an umbrella-frame.

In the collection of the Museum at Kaposvár are two reliefs in wood made by Péter Vörös, a swine-herd of Alsósegesd. One is 43 centimetres tall and is composed of two trees, with a squirrel and birds on the branches, and three deer between the trees. The other is 32 centimetres tall and shows Csáfor, an outlaw of Serbia, and Druzhina, his mistress (wife?), standing on either side of an oak-tree. Lajos Kara, who was not a herdsman but had learned carving from János Boszkovics, a herdsman of Buzsák, carved a scene of paradise on a board.

There are numerous figurative scenes and landscapes on the lids and sides of boxes decorated with raised work, as well as on the lids and bottoms of cigarette-boxes or mirror-cases. The compositions on such surfaces as

XIV Razor-case, Döbörhegy. Vas County, 1835

on the various utensils in general express the artist-herdsman's attempt within the limited space at his disposal to harmonize the realistic representation with the decoration of the whole.

The pieces we have mentioned here are really beyond the sphere of artistry characteristic of pastoral life, because the herdsmen-carvers had already left the limited world of their immediate environment. The inclination to carve, the manual skill, and the practice adjusted to changing circumstances, to new patterns, and the articles of the past gradually became ornaments detached from practical life and everyday activities.

Of these we must emphasize the small sculpture that appears on the lids of Transdanubian salt-cellars. Some of these carvers wrought animal figurines which showed artistic standards. The stylized ram, reminiscent of the prehistoric style, in the Museum of Szombathely is an outstanding example. Its counterpart, maybe its opposite, is in the Museum of Veszprém: this statuette, too, represents a ram, and surprises us by the keen observation and accuracy of realistic representation. Numerous carvings with religious themes were produced by the artist-herdsmen. Representations of Christ on the Cross are often found *(Plates 21, 22 and 23)*, and so are statu-

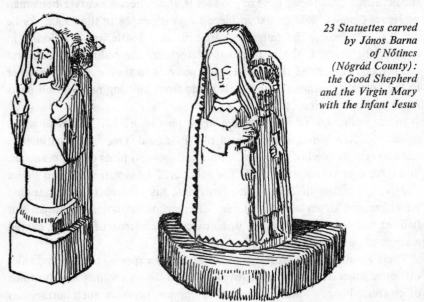

23 Statuettes carved by János Barna of Nőtincs (Nógrád County): the Good Shepherd and the Virgin Mary with the Infant Jesus

ettes no taller than a span, or a thumb, representing the Good Shepherd or the Blessed Virgin *(Fig. 23)*. These latter are characterized by an archaic primitivism of the style.

THE TECHNIQUES OF DECORATION

When discussing decorated articles, we have frequently referred to the technique in which geometric elements, flowers, human figures and animals ornamenting surfaces were carved.

As we have seen, the artist-herdsmen were skilled in a variety of techniques.

Since the techniques of decoration in many respects determine a given period of art, and are sometimes particular to a given region, by describing these we may begin to understand the artistic process and the significance of the motifs used. Above all, the technique of a decoration, together with the decoration itself, indicates the peculiarities of taste and the power of expression of the individual in whom traditions are preserved.

Chip Carving and Chiselling

As it has been shown, the earliest technique of decoration was the cutting of the lines and contours of patterns in superficial or deeper, narrower or wider grooves, with the latter occurring mainly in peasant carvings. This ancient technique was applied to certain objects until recently. Generally speaking, we can distinguish two methods in this technique: One is the decorative technique in which the linear ornamentation applied in wood or horn is formed by inclined incision executed by the point of the knife in two opposite directions. The other is notching or chip carving, another incised decoration of the surface, whose ornaments in general are geometrical patterns such as rosettes drawn with the help of a pair of compasses, sawteeth, angular curving lines and so on. These were applied by the carvers also as border decorations primarily on mangling boards, the sides of razor-cases and other objects.

Scratching

Scratching is a technique mainly used on articles made of horn; but it also occurs on articles of light-coloured wood, and on gourds. The carver cut a thin line into the surface with his knife, scratching in the pattern with the point of his blade. Flowers scratched in this manner were sometimes called *"filth flowers"* by the herdsmen of Transdanubia, because in the last century herdsmen often used the greasy layer of filth scraped from their hats to rub into the scratched lines to make the decoration stand out in sharp relief. They also used charcoal, coaldust, gunpowder and soot mixed with grease, axle-grease or burnt walnuts for this purpose. On horn, wood and gourds, scratched decorations or the backgrounds between them were sometimes stained yellow with *aqua fortis* (nitric acid).

A close inspection of decorations on horn, wood or gourds reveals that the thin scratched lines were used in combination with chip-carved wedge-cuts. Articles with this combined technique appear from the early years of the last century. This method was also used on the oldest salt-cellars and drinking-horns of the Great Plain and the region east of the Tisza.

Sealing-Wax Inlay

When we discussed the carvings of Transdanubia, we referred to the technique of sealing-wax ("Spanish wax") inlay. We also mentioned that the engraved decorations on mangling boards and razor-cases from the close of the eighteenth century and the beginning of the nineteenth century were sometimes rubbed with red paint, sometimes with sealing-wax or a black greasy substance. In the early use of sealing-wax, the carver-herdsmen melted wax instead of paint into the grooves by using a heated piece of metal or the point of a knife. We do not know when this technique became general in Hungary, but black and red wax were used to colour the incised decorations on razor-cases as early as the beginning of the last century. This technique might be called *wax intarsia* since a variant of this, similar to the technique of intarsia-work, was often employed in the middle of the century.

The second technique of sealing-wax inlay occurred both on wood and horn. The essence of this method is that the carver did not cut the contours of the patterns, but the background between, the "interstices", and filled these with wax. This permitted the use of a wider range of colours. We do not know if the herdsmen bought sealing-wax ready-made for use or produced it themselves. It is a fact, however, that they actually prepared coloured wax to colour their carvings. Two parts beeswax was melted in a vessel, one part of paint and a tenth of pine resin were added and then the mixture was boiled. When it cooled down and solidified, it was inserted into the carved grooves by means of a hot knife.

Metal, Horn and Bone Inlay

Decorative techniques similar to that of wax inlay were also employed by herdsmen carvers. In the first half of the last century, metal inlay was applied to whip-handles. The decorative elements such as sun, moon, stars, flowers, huts, etc. were cut out with scissors from a thin copper or brass sheet. They were attached to the surface to be decorated and their placement was marked. The shapes were then carved out and the metal forms were nailed back into the prepared indentations. Finally the nails and any protruding metal parts were filed even. About the end of the last century horn and bone inlay replaced copper and brass on the whip-handles, and after the turn of the century caoutchouc in various colours, taken from children's combs, appeared in inlay work. After the beginning of this century these techniques were also used increasingly on the herdsmen's sticks.

Tin Inlay

Whip-handles and sticks were also decorated with inlaid tin. The patterns, usually geometric, were carved in such a manner that the grooves met and terminated at the upper part of the stick or handle. When the carving was complete, the piece was wrapped in several layers of paper which formed a funnel-like extension beyond its upper end. Molten tin was poured into this paper device, and it ran along the grooves filling them and hardening in them as it cooled down. The tin was then sanded to a smooth finish. Tin required for this operation used to be obtained from cast-off tin vessels and later from the heads of soda-water bottles. Tin inlay served not only to decorate the stick or whip-handle, but also to increase the weight; which was useful for herdsmen.

Copper Plating

Brass and copper plating also served to decorate sticks, whip-handles and ax-helves. Three to four millimetres wide bands were cut from long sheets of brass and one edge was sharpened with a file. The band was then shaped to form angular or curving lines, stars, leaves, or flowers and was hammered into the wood. This technique was usually applied to handles made of plum-wood, because it was suitable for driving in thin plates. If the plates were thicker, an indentation into which they would fit was carved out beforehand. White alloy was also used in these cases. When the plates had been driven in, any protruding parts were filed off and then sanded smooth.

Carving in Relief

Raised or relief carving flourished most in Transdanubia in the latter half of the nineteenth century, although earlier it had been a favourite type of decoration on water dippers from the Uplands. The rudiments of the technique were already present in the type of waxing where the spaces between the patterns, i.e. the interstices, were chipped out. As a Transdanubian herdsman described he chipped away the wood between the flowers with his knife until the carved flower stood out from the background wood. Some herdsmen advocated this technique because they felt that the sealing-wax was not durable as it tended to drop out of the carved surfaces once the object was put to use.

When we inspect articles with relief carving more closely, we see that on older pieces this was only a result of removing the interstices which produced a relief-like representation. Raised woodwork proper or high relief, the plastic representation of decorations—which the herdsmen called *deeper carving*—reveals a more advanced practice. Plastic modelling required greater skill than the earlier techniques, and the differences appearing in this respect between carvers identify the work of the individual carver. The more plastic a decoration was, the more highly it was regarded. With raised woodwork, uneven spaces between the decorations were inevitably left. Carvers say that the roughness of these spaces was alleviated by piercing the interstices with the point of an awl or one that had been filed to a triangular shape. This procedure was called *pricking*. It is not found on old water dippers of the Uplands, but was common on them by the 1930s. A herdsman of Heves County, who for a while was engaged as a seasonal labourer in Veszprém County, learned this procedure in Transdanubia and introduced it to the Uplands.

In the application of any of the techniques we have discussed here, practice was of great importance. It can be observed how the technical skill of carvers improved with time and practice. Interruption of some years often resulted in a decline of skills.

THE DECORATIONS

As we have said by way of introduction, the vitality and vigour of an art is determined by the current and trends of change, even if the artistic activities of Hungarian herdsmen are characterized by a certain unity and constancy of style. The unity and constancy appear in the co-existence for long periods, and even amalgamation of elements that come from different cultural strata. Even so, one is able to trace the decline and eventual disappearance of certain elements, and to become aware of the emergence of new ones. The continuity of tradition in the art of the herdsmen consists in the very fact that past and present mingle without antagonism and then fuse in complete harmony. Older geometric elements fused with the rich floral ornamentation of the Renaissance and Baroque, with realistic flower representations later on, and reappear on nineteenth-century pastoral and brigand scenes, and religious and patriotic motifs; and they often emerge side by side with forms idiosyncratic to the carver or expressive of his social attitudes.

The stylistic marks of the art of carver-herdsmen were decisively determined—besides the carved object—by the decorative patterns in which the message, the contents and the aesthetic drive are realized. The combination and interrelationships of all these are the dominating feature of the carved objects, and they bear great emotional significance both for the artist and for the community to which he belongs. In a word, it is the patterns of decoration that carry the full context and meaning of the herdsman's work of art.

The early medieval stock of geometric patterns in European art was adopted as the basis of the decorative tradition of Hungarian folk art, particularly wood-carvings. This was a general development, perceivable in the folk art of other East European nations as well. It was this geometric heritage which, richly elaborated over the centuries, came to dominate Hungarian pastoral carving in the nineteenth century. Yet the arrangement and role of geometric elements underwent considerable changes. Decorations only appear in limited areas on the oldest wooden articles; on mangling boards, for example, they are seen in the centre of the surface, or near the handle. Apart from the Székely gates which are older, the decoration of the total surface of articles of everyday use appeared only in the second half of the eighteenth century. One might call it the second stage of decorative skill. During the nineteenth century, as floral motifs took over, the geometric elements were restricted to peripheral sites and only used as dividing lines, borders and closing forms of the ornaments. On mangling boards dating back to the late 1770s and early 1800s, the decorations filling the entire surface were *rosettes, stars in a circle, wheels with curved spokes, rotating wheels, teethings, sawteeth, angular and curving lines, hearts,* etc. On these mangling boards, one can see how the wheels with curved spokes and the rosettes were transformed into flowers, how unobtrusive foliage or flowers appeared occasionally here and there *(Plates 17 and 18)*.

The obsolescence of geometric elements and the gradual spread of floral ornamentation appear in the chiselled decorations on water dippers from southern Transdanubia and in the scratched decorations on horn articles of the Great Plain. The oldest dippers are decorated with chiselled rosettes, stars, semicircles and notches; on the more recent ones, only a few of these elements appear as border decorations. Geometric patterns *(Plate 6)* continue as ribbons, rings, fringes, and as borders and terminal ornamentation on whip-handles and staffs. Peasant carvings sporadically preserved the geometric elements; on the implements of spinning and weaving, on gate-posts, grave-posts, and chests they were often used in the last century.

The Stylized Flower

The great changes which gave rise to the richness and variation of floral representation in pastoral carving are related in several respects to partic- ular conditions in Transdanubia. Rural taste in this region was greatly influenced by its proximity to Western Europe and it tended to follow the great European styles. Needlework with carnations, pomegranates and the "Italian pitchers" are vigorous reminders of the Western patterns. The variety of peasant furniture surpassed that of other regions. The flowers in embroidery, painted furniture and glazed tiles not only stimulated the use of floral decoration in woodwork, but also influenced the arrangement of flowers on a given surface and within a given framework. The flowers, bunches of flowers in the square and oblong surfaces of furniture or glazed tiles provided examples for the composition of floral decoration on similar surfaces.

István Györffy, the great ethnographer of our century, writes that the ornamentation employed by furriers emerged some 150 years ago from realistic flower representation, and was conventionalized because the furriers imitated not natural flowers, but rather the flowers of the trade; in this way their ornamentation of realistic origin changed and was simplified by passing it from hand to hand. This decoration had an influence on pastoral carvings throughout the nineteenth century, especially in the full development of the rich variety of waxed flower decorations.

"The floral elements and birds of the frieze-cloaks of the Bakony mountains," Györffy writes, "remind us of the waxed decorations of Transdanubian pastoral carvings. If we know that the Transdanubian herdsman was very fond of carving himself and his cloaked companions, we cannot doubt that he took the decorative elements, even the decorations proper, for his scratched green or red sealing-wax inlaid mirror-cases, razor-cases, etc., from his frieze-cloak first of all. The trimmings of this cloak were always before his eyes." *(Plate XII.)* László Madarassy tells us that the originals of the delicately composed notchings on the drinking-horns of the Upper Tisza region are to be found on the adorned tobacco pouches made of ram's scrotum, frieze-cloaks and sheepskin coats. The rose is nothing else—he writes—but the leather rosette that holds the strap of the clip on the embroidered frieze-cloak; this rosette is made up of three or four layers of crenated circular pieces. And this rose occurs chiefly as the central decoration amid stylized flowers and leaves.

To accept these statements at face value would be to oversimplify the question of floral representation in Hungarian pastoral carving. The artist-herdsman never copied the patterns he saw outright. When he saw a form that he considered beautiful, it inspired him to create, to call into being something new, and the new was inevitably different from the original inspiration. It could not be the same, because it was conceived differently and produced by imagination with a different technique, in a different material, in different circumstances, and filtered through different experiences and emotional associations. In addition we must consider the models, the influences as a matter of course if we are to get some inside view of the rich realm of the creative herdsman's imagination, of the process of inspiration and production.

One frequent pattern in the Transdanubian pastoral carvings is a stylized flower, or bunch of flowers, placed in vessels of various forms and reminiscent of flowers of the "Italian pitcher" *(Plate 18)*. Often with vertical or transversal compositions the garland-like flower emerged from a heart placed in one corner of the border *(Fig. 9)*. The flower, or bunch of flowers, held in the bill by a bird, or a pair of birds, or placed between birds, can be traced back to ancient traditions and beliefs. Besides these two widely spread types the flower motif recurs in countless other, often quite idiosyncratic variants of representation and arrangement. The pattern relies, for the most part, on the Baroque ornamental tradition as it developed on painted furniture, glazed tiles, and painted panels. The ideal of ornamentation is decorativeness. The style adapted itself to cylindrical surfaces as well. While on flat surfaces the flower bunch dominates, on staffs and whip-handles garlands of flowers and foliage, more adaptable to space, are favoured.

The Realistic Flower

If we ask herdsmen about the flowers carved by them, we usually hear two opinions. Some of the Transdanubian herdsmen summed up their feelings like this: they had never seen anything like the flowers they carved; or "the real flower is the one that does not grow, but is invented by somebody". This opinion evidently refers to the stylized flowers we have mentioned in the preceding chapter. By contrast, other carvers called the flowers they carved by name: field or wild flowers, Catherine flower, white lily, rosemary, stonecrop, camomile, Saint George's flower, tulip, tea rose, geranium, clover-leaf, acacia leaves, etc. One carver, criticizing stylized flowers, remarked: "...I have never seen a flower from whose stalk a tulip and a rose bloomed at the same time." This herdsman emphasized that whenever he depicted a forest he only carved trees and acorns on the surface to be decorated, because there were no flowers in the forest. This remark is indicative of efforts to represent the herdsman's environment, the trees and flowers realistically.

Mihály Tóth, a carver of Felsősegesd in Somogy County, says that he saw some of his flowers on old carvings; the others he gathered in fields and forests. When he began carving, he picked several field flowers, examined them, sketched them, then carved or incised them in wood. He recalled that his father, who had been to Tyrol during the Great War, had brought home an edelweiss and scratched it upon his salt-cellars. Speaking of the old herdsmen—from whom he also had learned much—he said that they used to carve tulips simply because there were tulips on their chests. "One carved only tulips, nothing else, the other only wild roses because those were his favourites." On another occasion Mihály Tóth said: "We do not want flowers to be natural, they should be as fanciful as possible. Flowers and leaves intermingled." The apparent contradiction between these and the former statements is resolved by the eclectic taste of the carver; Mihály Tóth saw part of his flowers on old carvings, and collected the rest from the field.

In the carver's mind, in the world of his imagination, a multitude of images accumulated. It was there that the decorations he had seen in the carvings of his predecessors and teachers lived, united and mixed with patterns he had seen elsewhere, on objects, in books or in nature. In the last analysis, his floral representations were determined by the large store of these images and by his individuality. The more intense the will to create something new and different, the more the carver departed from the usual, from the restricted forms, the closer he got to what he held to be natural. Because he wanted to fill a given space as fully as possible and also to conform to pastoral tastes, he could not realize a realistic representation and had instead to choose a solution which employed both stylized and realistic floral elements.

In such a way what was considered as "not true" and "not real" merged

68 harmoniously with what was "true" and "real". It was exactly this trait that endowed the herdsmen's art with such vitality, gave rise to changes, and made the role of the individual decisive in creation.

Although we feel that we must point to the prototypes of the herdsmen's floral representations, we shall not attempt to find the concrete manifestations of the historical style of different periods in the flowers of his carvings. We will not, therefore, investigate where the carver took this or that decorative element or pattern from. There is no doubt that the carvers conformed in their adoption of certain elements, but even so it is not a case of sameness, of articles being identical, but of resemblance, and they are not really related in most cases. Although they emerged from similar traditions, similar perceptions and experience, they are manifestly independent of one another.

It is not chiefly in the decorative elements, not in ornamentation by itself, that we look for the characteristics of the herdsman's artistic creations; it is rather in the relations of these elements to the object, the implement, to the surface to be decorated, and in the particularities of their application. Although the aesthetic conventions of the community were quite commanding, still, as we have seen, the artist's individual imagination, the personal contents of his consciousness and his creative ability played a decisive role. The delicate interplay of the demands of utility, of conventions and individual talent thus determines ornamentation both in its motifs and construction so that every work, in its entirety and its details alike, becomes a unique reformulation.

Birds and Animals of Field and Forest

Amid flowers and floral ornamentation we often find portrayals of birds; these also preserve ancient traditions. At the close of the seventeenth century, a tulip and two birds above a cut-out heart were carved on the back of a chair made for Ferenc Rákóczi II. Two birds facing each other and a flower between them also occur on the lid of a razor-case made at the end of the eighteenth century. Birds standing on flowers, holding a flower in their bills, facing each other on either sides of floral designs, occurred frequently from the middle of the last century on.

Herdsmen often portrayed a dove with a flower in its bill. It was regarded as a symbol of love and affection. One man told us that when his wife was in hospital he carved a kerchief-rack for her and decorated it with two wild pigeons billing. He thought that if she came home cured she would rejoice in the gift—and if she died this carving would always remind him of her. Other popular birds were the thrush, the wild turtle-dove, and the hoopoe. Birds with a topknot and crest on their heads were usually identified with the latter.

What had been said about the relationship of stylized and realistic flowers is also applicable to the representations of birds. We know of space-filling compositions—especially in Transdanubia—where birds were parts of a stylized flower ornament, where emphasis was placed on the representation as a whole, on the decorative pattern of the surface, and not on details. It seems probable that, among others, the trimmings of the embroidered frieze-cloak contributed to their preservation. Unlike other Hungarian frieze-cloaks, those of the Bakony region sometimes had figural decorative elements. The most frequent was the bird, usually portrayed as a dove or a swallow. The dove holds a flower in its bill, the swallow carries a leaf. We often see bird representations which do not serve the purpose of decorative structural solutions, but grew out of the desire to depict them realistically. Such are the birds flying, perching, sitting in the nest, etc. One herdsman incised a scene on his horn he had seen somewhere: a bird brooding in its nest is about to fly off because it is afraid of a snake that is creeping up the tree. We have seen an eagle with a hare in its claws.

We see attempts to depict the environment on utensils, where the carving is of the trees of the forest, the animals of the herd such as the ram, the sheep, the pig, the cattle; the dog, or the herdsman's hut. The favourite motif of herdsmen in the woodlands is the stag, the roe-deer. They had seen them on plates and jugs, in hunting scenes, then they incised and scratched them on their decorated utensils, either as mere decorative elements of the ornamental structure, or for their own sake as the concrete symbols of a memorable experience. Stags, roe-deers, hunters, squirrels sitting on a tree, foxes on the prowl, rams, pigs with the swine-herd, etc. were carved especially on boxes made for sale.

A snake coiling around a stick or pipe-stem, carved in relief, is a feature peculiar to Transdanubia. The motif has its models, and it is perhaps related to that rich cycle of beliefs about snakes once held in Transdanubia. The relief carvings themselves occurred rather late and were preceded by what was evidently a very old practice of drawing the skin of a snake onto a stick to make it "fanciful". It seems probable that in the past some belief was attached to such a stick.

Snakes were frequently shown holding a frog in the mouth. Herdsmen said that grass snakes lived on frogs, and that is why they carved the frog with one or both hind legs in the mouth of the snake. This scene is also connected with the belief that if a herdsman saves a frog from a snake, he will be forgiven the seven deadly sins. Hence we believe that the portrayal of the snake made its way into the decorations of sticks on the basis of existing models, to become later on, in combination with the frog, the illustration of that older belief.

Herdsmen, Outlaws

The most conspicuous feature of Hungarian pastoral carvings is the representation of herdsmen and outlaws. Actually, herdsmen and outlaws belong together in folk imagination, because, as the herdsmen hold, it was the herdsmen that turned outlaws. True, other elements mixed with outlaws, but those who became notorious were of pastoral origin. From the findings of ethnographers it appears that the representation of the human form, of herdsmen and outlaws in particular, on Transdanubian carvings occurred more and more often from the 1830s on *(Plate 29)*. The earliest portrayals appear on razor-cases and mirror-cases; later on they were applied to various other utensils. All these attempted to portray the characters realistically, detailing the style of the hair and moustache, the various articles of clothing, the ax, the shepherd's crook, or the gun; by a dexterity of stylization, a clever spatial arrangement of the figures, by the unity and harmony of composition aimed at filling up surfaces. At the same time, most of these representations show a variety of scenes taken from the herdsmen's and outlaws' lives, their legendary deeds, sometimes their unhappy end, or their drinking-bouts.

Although the roots of brigandage in Hungary date back much farther, the increase in the early years of the last century must be ascribed to circumstances prevailing at that time. The despotism of county authorities became worse in the early 1800s. Officials, district administators treated the serfs inhumanely, and often inflicted corporal punishment in person slapping the face, flogging, lashing, caning. Manorial courts arrested and took into custody whomever they liked. Most prisons and gaols were nothing but filthy underground caves. So it is understandable that the herdsmen took refuge in forests after getting into trouble with the authorities. In the beginning, hiding compelled them to commit petty thefts; but later on they robbed, and even committed murder to escape, or simply out of revenge. In this way they cut off the possibility of return once and for all. The only way to avoid imprisonment was to go on hiding.

Many herdsmen hid to avoid impressment, or because they had deserted. At that time, military service in foreign lands sometimes lasted twelve years, and it was no better there than under the despotism of the county officials. Many men had endured a hundred and fifty strokes in the army before they joined the outlaws. At the close of the eighteenth and in the early years of the nineteenth century, peasant movements, and antifeudal revolts were set afoot in Transdanubia, directed against the taking back of logged land, and against excessive demands on socage. Expropriation of land, the extension of arable areas, protection of forest—all resulted in restrictions imposed on herdsmen and their pastoral life. This gave rise to embitterment, and to resistance to exploitation and oppression. All this was heightened by the fact that outlaws maintained regular contacts with herdsmen and with the peasantry of the region, and often avoided the gallows or imprisonment—if only for a short time—through the protection or shelter offered by these.

Old Transdanubian carver-herdsmen invariably remembered the outlaws of the past by name. Most of them even recalled the important episodes of the outlaws' life, and not only portrayed them, but justified it. We often heard this intention: "Almost all of these carvings show former outlaws—they were carved by swine-herds, shepherds, who had known them, and emulating these, we portrayed them so that their eternal fame should survive." Some of them said: "Herdsmen regarded the outlaw as a righteous man, because he did no harm to the poor, he only worked against the squires; that is why their figures, the events told about them, were carved in wood, because they were proud of them." In the course of conversations these outlaws were often mentioned by name: Jóska Sobri, András Juhász, Pista Séta, Jóska Savanyú, Pista Patkó were famous men, afraid of nobody. One shepherd of Somogy County explained his outlaw-representations like this: "Our ancestors told us what kind of people these outlaws had been, what apparel they wore. When I was six, five of them came to see my father. They were fine men, wearing frieze-cloaks, the rifles hanging on their necks, the small axes from their left arms, they wore boots, and had wide linen trousers, with a broad belt at the waist with a pistol, cartridges and knives on it. They also wore a close-fitting dolman—they looked like the ones I am carving."

Not only herdsmen and outlaws, but also females appear in pastoral carvings. The carvers told us how to interpret such scenes: a shepherd boy is chatting with his sweetheart, or a young wife offers wine to the herdsman. We also find dancing scenes, such as the illustration of the ballad about the girl danced to death: Mariska Sági was the mistress of outlaws, and because she betrayed them, they danced with her until she died. Records and stories recall that the outlaws had sweethearts who accompanied them, and with whom they caroused. Old Antal Kapoli explained the figures scratched on one of his salt-cellars as follows: "On most of them there are these women-folk, Bori Dombi, Treszka Kulcsár, Böske Bödő. The latter died with a rifle in her hand when her house was surrounded by the gendarmes."

Patriotic and Other Motifs

In the 1820s strains of political and economic nature developed between the Hungarian nobility and Vienna. Although erratic and vacillating, Hungarian gentry joined the fight for national independence. Changes in politics were marked by a growing national resistance in the circles of nobility and citizenry. From the early 1820s until the outbreak of the War of Independence, progressive forces in Hungary confronted a twofold task: opposing the Austrian colonizers and the forces of feudalism, in other words to attain independence and to further bourgeois progress. These aspirations manifested themselves in different ways, and presented themselves in various forms in all walks of life.

The hussars and outlaws on the honey-cakes, decorations with Hungarian

XV Razor-case, inlaid with sealing-wax, 1824 ▷

historical motifs on articles of everyday use produced for the citizenry and nobility, the outlaws in the trashy paperbacks—all these expressed this aspiration. More decorations with patriotic motifs were produced after the defeat of 1849, during the Bach administration. Woodwork enthusiasts, artisans, commoners, county officials were carving sticks and pipe-stems covering them with scenes taken from Hungary's history. A carver named András Bagol incised on the pipe-stems, on ax-helves, crooks and sticks he carved historical portraits such as those of Sándor Petőfi, the poet of the 1848 Revolution, and of leading statesman Lajos Kossuth. The scenes were accompanied with inscriptions such as "Arrival of the Conquering Magyars", "The Siege of Szigetvár", "Sándor Rózsa the Scourge of God", "Rise Hungarians!"

These and other illustrations of patriotic, historic import made their impression on the herdsmen engaged in carving: the opposition to Habsburg rule, the revolutionary ideals of '48, took roots in pastoral communities. As a result of all this, it was fairly common practice in the 1850s for carvers to picture the Kossuth Arms of Hungary. On sticks of that time we often see, beside or below the arms, inscriptions such as "Memento of 1848", lines of "Rise Hungarians!" and, again, portraits of Petőfi or Kossuth. Patriotic motifs were often used later, at the turn of the century. In addition to those mentioned, there were depictions of Ferenc Rákóczi II, of the Seven Conquering Princes, of the Compact sealed with blood. At the time of the Great War, a swine-herd of Báta (Tolna County) incised his horn with the Russian Czar and Wilhelm II with their sabres drawn, about to fight on horseback, while the King of Hungary tries to appease them. Reality and the elements of fables were linked in this way.

Some carvers tried their hand at illustrating tales. The swine-herd of Szepezd (Zala County) scratched upon his horn Prince Árgirus killing the twelve-headed dragon, and portrayed also Fairy Helen. The maker of a salt-cellar carved in the lid a swine-herd warming himself at a fire, similar to the scene on the ace of diamonds. Representations with religious motifs were no rarity on articles made in the last century. Mangling boards were sometimes decorated with altars, crosses, candlesticks, and images of the Holy Virgin. A razor-case dated 1826 was decorated with the monstrance, two candlesticks and the chalice. The scene in paradise, showing Adam and Eve with the forbidden fruit and the serpent between them, occurs

XVI Field-guard's ax. Paszab, Szabolcs-Szatmár County, 1846

on sticks and other articles. On the one side of a mirror-case from 1840 two outlaws are shaking hands, while there is an altar on the other side. The carver had evidently seen no contradiction between these scenes. There are mirror-cases, of course, where images of a religious theme were carved on both sides. Among these we find the church of some place of pilgrimage, the image of the Holy Virgin, etc.

There were religious men among the herdsmen; they carried prayer books and devotional pictures on them, and visited places of pilgrimage. Their creations of religious nature certainly had emotional foundations, but in most cases it was only the interest of a picture that attracted them; icons in a church or illustrations in religious books.

It cannot be emphasized strongly enough—and this can be followed on objects—that even if these elements and decorations seem only to keep interchanging in the course of years, they actually change constantly. They are like the waves of the sea, one diving to the depths, the other emerging on the surface—yet what had gone down was replaced by something else, and what reappeared on the surface was not what it had been. And then came newer and newer waves. The herdsman's everyday life fluctuated and changed and as his experience grew, his decorations changed. However powerful habit may be, its constancy is relative, for it is gradually formed and reshaped by the innumerable events of life, by the multitude of perceptions and emotions.

Through the carved articles we have presented we can observe how the variety of plastic forms and the desire for decoration gained ground. The newer techniques preserved much of the old decorative elements, but there was increasingly more of the new. As the new techniques spread, the close relationship between the way of life and the art loosened. It was no longer the utilitarian value of the article that mattered, it was the decoration. Decoration was no longer to enhance the article. The article existed for the decoration. Thus in the last decades the old-time carvers, having abandoned their pastoral life, and the new carvers who never knew such a life, no longer carved the utensils of the past, of the ancient mode of life.

Yet even so those book-stands, various boxes, cigarette-holders, ashtrays, glass-stands no longer carved by herdsmen preserve the traditions of pastoral art: they have retained the forms of things, the decorative techniques and the decorative patterns.

SUMMARY

From all we have said in the preceding chapters we can draw the conclusion that this off-shoot of Hungarian folk art which began in the early years of the nineteenth century grew into a wide-branching tree during the course of one century. Together with Ottó Herman, its first researcher, we may rightly call it "herdsmen's art", because the majority of the decorated articles are accessories of herding life; and because the skill of herdsmen practising art made the decorative techniques and patterns expressive of the way of life, ways of thinking and tastes of this peculiar social stratum.

The carver-herdsman's vocabulary of forms was drawn from three sources. One was the totality of decorative elements and decorations which he had seen on the decorated objects of his predecessors, which stimulated him to action, and inspired him to create. The other source was the techniques, decorations and representations which he had seen on creations of non-pastoral origin, and which had captured his interest and attention. The third, the richest source was his own environment, everyday life, the herd, nature itself, and the multitude of images and phenomena he observed in nature.

From all these he chose and selected when creating compositions to decorate his utensils, and in realizing his choice he conformed to his and his community's taste and ideas and used his skill and talent for the portrayal.

The way of life, his work, and the potentialities of representation kept the herdsman's artistry, his dexterity of expression, in bounds; so it was a natural consequence that certain forms, decorative elements and compositions became popular, habitual and frequent, and that it was these that served as the commonest themes for his portrayals. But these did not recur mechanically: he shaped and formed the old ones, complementing them with new elements. The carver's attitude, range of emotions, which determined his relation to his community and his artistry alike, was revealed in his activites. Hence the possibilities of representation were limited and determined by a few circumstances that can be summed up as follows.

Firstly, the examples he had seen—which may be called tradition—which served to guide the carver in the representation and formal execution of an incessantly growing body of experience. They showed how to reduce phenomena and objects of complex appearance to make them expressive of attached ideas and emotional content, to make them suitable for expressing the phenomena, the objects selected for portrayal.

Secondly, the properties of the materials and the surfaces to be decorated, determined rendering, its possibilities and dimensions, the relative proportions of certain decorative elements, constituent parts, relations which did not follow the natural, but gave prominence to what he wanted to emphasize.

Finally, the skill of representation, whose components were shaped by ambition, creative imagination, and practice.

All these combined to exert a decisive influence on what the artist-herdsman selected from the multitude of phenomena surrounding him, and from the mass of experience that affected and impressed him; they also influenced which of these phenomena and experiences he was able to portray.

The carver-herdsman knew as well as anybody else—and this has often been referred to—that nature, the images seen, experiences and ideas were not always suited to his means of expression. We often heard remarks that this or that "cannot be incised" or "cannot be carved in wood". But even within existing limits there were innumerable opportunities for choice, and the manner in which it was made was always characteristic of the carver's personality. We knew herdsmen who only carved flowers, or oak-leaves and acorns; we knew carvers who portrayed, in addition to these, outlaws, scenes of pastoral life, historical, patriotic events, or even scenes from tales. We knew some who only varied familiar forms, incised or carved lifeless, stylized flowers; and others whose ambition it was to portray environment, flowers, trees, and flocks realistically.

All these examples emphasize the relationship between the art and the way of life and indicate the collective features of its function, the individual traits of rendering. Essentially, pastoral art is the art of a community; its style, basic technical and decorative characteristics are homogeneous. Yet as concerns the talent for expression, the message and the contents, it has as many shades, as many aspects as there were individual carvers. No carver ever repeated the same decoration in exactly the same manner; but if we observe the technique, the decorative elements, the manner of composition of some of his creations, we are able to identify the maker because certain familiar features of his technique of representation, the characteristic forms of portrayal, and the message his portrayal wishes to convey, betray the personality of their creator.

The aim of folk art—including that of the herdsman—is to produce beautiful things, beautiful implements. Whenever attempts were made to shape an object or a decoration considered as beautiful, these attempts were subject to the realities of the world around, of nature, environment, of the herdsman's everyday life. The realism of art, of the decorations, lies exactly in this: for the image of reality, arranged by the artist-herdsman's way of thinking and judgment, appears in his representations, in this harmony of practicality and beauty. Expression of the message takes place by using the real, the seen, and imaginary images. But even the non-real, the imaginary, was created from components of reality. That is why the forms produced by imagination are also real in a sense, and always speak to their creator and his community. And the use and application of the seen, of the real, just as of the imaginary, are governed by the laws of the artist-herdsman's cast of mind, scope of emotions, attitude towards the outside world, and his taste.

In folk art great importance is attributed to tradition. Indeed, the force of tradition must not be underestimated. Yet tradition alone explains neither the force of forms and decorations, nor their vitality and survival. It is the circumstances of life, change and variability that determine survival and continuity. As long as the identity of a way of life persisted, decorated articles increased in number; techniques and decorations became more and more varied; as soon as herdsmanship declined, the thread of artistry began to thin out. After all, tradition was kept alive by the necessity of useful objects and implements. What we have to emphasize is that the living tradition of forms never repeats itself unchanged, and that even in a seemingly repeated form it is never the former that is realized anew. There is a statement which applies to pastoral art as well: "In tradition we cannot speak of a non-recurring, final form, nor of a non-recurring, final content that must be 'reproduced' in great numbers once it had been created. The reproduction, retelling, resinging of handed-down tradition is a lesser or greater alteration of retold contents and forms at the same time."

Some writers stress that it is exactly in the field of pastoral art, where stylistic influences are the least likely, that we see an astonishing kinship of the art of all peoples of Europe. This kinship exists indeed, it is inseparable from the similarity in ways of life; yet in our discussion we have seen the dissimilar, particular Hungarian historical antecedents, different circumstances of life, different social and cultural environment, which produced dissimilarities, the "different" as a matter of necessity. And it is in this difference, in these dissimilarities, produced and shaped by a Hungarian past, Hungarian soil that we must search for, and can find, all that is particularly Hungarian in our pastoral art.

BIBLIOGRAPHY

Bátky, Zsigmond: *Pásztor ivópoharak* [Drinking-Cups of Shepherds]. Budapest, **79** 1928.

Bátky–Györffy–Viski: *Magyar népművészet* [Hungarian Folk Art]. Budapest, 1928.

Bednarik, R.: *Pastierské rezbárske umenie*. Bratislava, 1956.

Béres, András: "A Déri Múzeum Debrecen környéki díszes pásztorbotjai" [Ornamental Shepherd's Crooks of the Debrecen Area in the Déri Museum]. *Year-Book of the Debrecen Déri Museum*, 1960–61.

Domanovszky, György: *A két faragó Kapoli* [The Two Carver Kapolis]. Budapest, 1955.

Fél–Hofer–Csilléry: *Hungarian Peasant Art*. Budapest, 1969.

Fél, Edit–Hofer, Tamás: *Saints, Soldiers, Shepherds*. Budapest, 1966.

Füzes, Endre: "A Janus Pannonius Múzeum borotvatartói" [Razor-Cases in the Janus Pannonius Museum]. *Year-Book of the Janus Pannonius Museum*, Pécs, 1961.

Györffy, István: *Magyar népi hímzések*. I. *A cifraszűr* [Hungarian Folk Embroideries. I. The Embroidered Frieze-Cloak]. Budapest, 1930.

Herman, Ottó: *Az ősfoglalkozások. Halászat és pásztorélet* [Ancient Occupations. Fishing and Shepherding]. Reprint. Budapest, 1898.

Lükő, Gábor: "A hortobágyi pásztorművészet" [Shepherds' Art in Hortobágy]. *Year-Book of the Debrecen Déri Museum*, 1938.

Madarassy, László: *Vésett pásztortülkök* [Incised Shepherd's Horns]. Budapest, 1925.

Madarassy, László: *Művészkedő magyar pásztorok* [Hungarian Shepherd Artists]. Budapest, 1934.

A magyarság néprajza [Ethnography of the Hungarians]. Vol. II. Budapest, no date.

Malonyay, Dezső: *A magyar nép művészete*. III. *A Balaton melléke* [The Art of the Hungarian People. III. The Balaton Region]. Budapest, no date.

Manga, János: "Betjarendarstellungen auf den Schnitzereien ungarischer Hirten." *Acta Ethn.*, 1951.

Manga, János: *Egy dunántúli faragó pásztor* [A Transdanubian Shepherd Carver]. Budapest, 1954.

Manga, János: "Hirtenkunst in Transdanubien." *Acta Ethn.*, 1961.

Manga, János: "Hirtenkunst im Tiefland und im Oberland." *Acta Ethn.*, 1967.

Ortutay, Gyula: *A magyar nép művészete* [The Art of the Hungarian People]. Vols. I–II. Budapest, 1941.

Tombor, Ilona: *Old Hungarian Painted Woodwork*. Budapest, 1967.

Tombor, Ilona: *Magyarországi famennyezetek és rokonemlékek a XV–XIX. századból* [Hungarian Wooden Ceilings and Similar Remains from the 15th to 19th Centuries]. Budapest, 1968.

80

LIST OF BLACK AND WHITE PLATES

1 *Antal Kapoli sen.*, carver-herdsman, Kossuth Prize winner. Born in 1867 at Kisgyalán, Somogy County. Started to look after animals at the age of 10 helping his elder brother. Became a contract shepherd when 26. Moved to his own house in the neighbourhood of Somogyhárságy when he turned 64 and worked as a carver till his death in 1957.

2 *Lajos Garai*, horse-herd of Máta (Hortobágy), decorating a whip-handle (1963).

3 *Mihály Tóth*, carver-herdsman, 1943. Born in 1911 at Somogyliszó. Out with animals from early childhood. In 1938 he became a head shepherd and moved to his present home at Lászlómajor, near Felsősegesd. In the past fifteen years he has spent most of his time doing carving.

4 *József Ostoróczki*, carver-herdsman of Egercsehi, Heves County. 1951.

5 *Carver's knives* decorated with tin-work. From southern Transdanubia (right and left) and Nógrád County (centre). Length 16.5 to 18.5 cm. Ethnographical Museum, Budapest.

6 *Whip-handles*, with cast tin, metal inlay, brass-plated and carved ornaments, from the 1900s and 1920s. Length 38 to 46 cm. King Stephen Museum, Székesfehérvár.

7 *Shepherd's crook*, with ram's head and floral ornamentation. Length 91 cm. Balaton Museum, Keszthely.

8 *Shepherd's crook*, mountain-ash, with ram's head carved by Mihály Zöld. Turn of the century. Length 110.5 cm. Provenance: Dunaadony-Dajapuszta, Fejér County King Stephen Museum, Székesfehérvár.

9 *Shepherd's stick*, mountain-ash, carved in relief, dated 1899. Length 92 cm, handle 16.5 cm. King Stephen Museum, Székesfehérvár.

10 *Shepherd's crook*, ash root, with dragon's head at the end of the crook. Length 107 cm. Provenance: Csapod, Győr-Sopron County. Ferenc Liszt Museum, Sopron.

11 *Shepherd's crook*, for festive occasions, with human figure sitting on the crooked end. Dated 1888. Length 110 cm. Provenance: Csákvár, Fejér County. King Stephen Museum, Székesfehérvár.

12 *Shepherd's crook*, mountain-ash, with human head on the top of the crook and ram's head at the end of the crook. Length 107 cm. Carved by János Berdi, a shepherd, early in the 20th century. Provenance. Csákberény, Fejér County. King Stephen Museum, Székesfehérvár.

13 *Razor-case*, with red and black sealing-wax inlay. Dated 1842 (at top end).

A shepherd in an embroidered frieze-cloak, wearing Sobri-style hat, smoking his pipe and holding a shepherd's crook, is shown on the lid. Length of case 21 cm. Provenance: Bakonybél, Veszprém County. Bakony Museum, Veszprém.

14 *Razor-case*, maple, with sealing-wax-inlaid green and red floral ornamentation, dated 1854. Length 25 cm. Provenance: Nagycenk, Győr-Sopron County. Ferenc Liszt Museum, Sopron.

15 *Shaving-mirror frame*, with decoration carved in relief. Height 31 cm. Ferenc Liszt Museum, Sopron.

16 *Shaving-mirror case*, with red, green and black sealing-wax inlay on the back. A swine-herd in an embroidered frieze-cloak is on the right with a Somogy swine-herd's ax on his shoulder. An outlaw with his sweetheart on the left. He carries a gun on his shoulder and a powder-horn in his left hand. Made in the 1870s. Length 17 cm. Ethnographical Museum, Budapest.

17 *Mangling boards with engraved decoration*. The one on the right (Bakony Museum, Veszprém) was made in 1770, the one on the left (Ferenc Liszt Museum, Sopron) in 1829.

18 *Details of the decoration of a mangling board*. An inscription below the man's figure with a violin and the pair of dancers states: "Made by Zsiga Károly for Eörzsébet Kiss." Ferenc Liszt Museum, Sopron.

19 *Swine-herd's ax of Somogy County*, the helve decorated with sealing-wax inlay. Ethnographical Museum, Budapest.

20 *Herdsmen's sticks*, top decorated with cast tin. The one on the left comes from Szarvas, Békés County. There are calluses on the stick in the middle: before lopping off the twig for the stick, the maker had punctured it with an awl or knife. Provenance: Kazár, Nógrád County. The stick on the right was made in 1860. Ethnographical Museum, Budapest.

21 *Cross*, pear-wood. Height 18.5 cm. Carved by János Barna, a shepherd of Nőtincs, Nógrád County, in the early years of the 20th century. Palóc Museum, Balassagyarmat.

22 *Cross*, plum-wood. Carved in the 1930s by János Havran, a swine-herd of Kisterenye, Nógrád County. Height about 16 cm. Palóc Museum, Balassagyarmat.

23 *Aspersorium*, carved of maple-wood. A stylized Virgin Mary surrounded by flowers is under the cross. Carved in relief. Height 18.5 cm. Balaton Museum, Keszthely.

24 *Salt-cellar*, coloured with red, black, blue and yellow sealing-wax. On the one side is the figure of a man and a woman, on the other floral ornamentation and foliage. Made in 1895. Height 9.8 cm. Provenance: Somogy County. Balaton Museum, Keszthely.

25 *Salt-cellar*, with scratched decorations. A herdsman in wide linen pantaloons, wearing a dolman and a Sobri-style hat, embracing two women, is on one side and three outlaws with guns are on the other. Height 8 cm. Göcsej Museum, Zalaegerszeg.

26 *Salt-cellar*, with red, blue and green sealing-wax-inlaid flowers. Made late in the 1930s by János Boszkovics, a herdsman of Buzsák, Somogy County. Height 5.5 cm. Private collection.

27 *Match-box*, with a man's and a woman's figure carved in relief, coloured, with foliage and floral ornamentation. Height 7.7 cm. Carved in the late 1930s by János Boszkovics, a herdsman of Buzsák, Somogy County. Private collection.

28 *Match-box*, with lids opening at both ends. The light-yellow, red, green and maroon sealing-wax-inlaid decoration shows the lamb as a Christian symbol. The initials of the maker, Ignác Zöld, a shepherd of Szúnyogpuszta, Veszprém County, are in the left corner. Length 7 cm. Made in 1908. Bakony Museum, Veszprém.

29 *Mirror-case*, with red and black sealing-wax inlay. The picture carved on the sliding lid is, according to tradition, supposed to show a soldier sent to get Jóska Sobri who is on bent knees in front of the notorious outlaw begging for his life. Length 10.4 cm. Dated 1840. Provenance: Magyargencs, Vas County. Ethnographical Museum, Budapest.

30 *Match-box*, with lids opening at both ends. The bird on the branch and the border are in blue, white, yellow, red, brown, pink and bluish-grey sealing-wax-work. Length 7 cm. Made in 1909, by Mihály Liszák, a shepherd of Szúnyogpuszta. Bakony Museum, Veszprém.

31 *Bench*, the nine pierced panels on the black show soldiers, mounted hussars, and scenes of pastoral life. Made in 1910. Provenance: Nógrád County. Palóc Museum, Balassagyarmat.

32 *Watch-chain*, carved from horn, length 32.5 cm. Balaton Museum, Keszthely.

33 *Horn*, decorated by scratching. The spaces in the pattern are coloured yellow with nitric acid. Stylized floral ornamentation surrounds the figures of an outlaw, a herdsman and a hunter. There are oak-trees, acorns and birds. The date 1948 and the surname of the maker, Antal Kapoli sen., appear over the decorated part. Length 33 cm. Private collection.

34 *Detail of the horn on Plate 33*. According to Antal Kapoli sen., the figure represents András Juhász, a shepherd turned outlaw.

35 *Gourd*, with scratched decorations, the spaces between coloured yellow with nitric acid. The main figure is a shepherd, with a shepherd's crook in his hand. Made by Antal Kapoli sen. Height 17.5 cm. Balaton Museum, Keszthely.

36 *Scab-grease case*, horn, with scratched decorations coloured yellow. The principal figure is a shepherd on a donkey's back, holding a crook. Height 9 cm. Provenance: Okány, Békés County. Ethnographical Museum, Budapest.

37 *Water dipper*, pear-wood, with decorations carved in relief. The handle shows a dog. Length 12 cm. Provenance: Nógrád County. Palóc Museum, Balassagyarmat.

38 *Water dipper*, plum-wood, decorations carved in relief. The handle is a snake and a roe, on the side of the cup is an oak-tree, a roe-deer, fox, pig and a flying bird. Made in the 1930s by József Ostoróczki, a cowherd of Heves County. Private collection.

39 *Water dipper*. Dentate border ornamentation surrounds a shepherd and a hunter carved in relief. Two carved human figures facing each other are on the handle. The initials H. J. and the date 1930 are carved at the bottom. Length 17 cm. Made in 1930 by József Hajnák, a shepherd of Zagyvapálfalva, Nógrád County. Palóc Museum, Balassagyarmat.

40 *Water dipper*, plum-wood, the decorations carved in relief show oak-leaves, tulips, a swine-herd with an ax, and a hunter. A carved pig serves as the handle. Made in the 1940s by János Barna, who was then a swine-herd at Kisterenye, Nógrád County. Length 13.5 cm. Palóc Museum, Balassagyarmat.

41 *Salt and paprika-cellar*, with sliding lid, divided into four compartments, with four small legs at the bottom. Decorated with sealing-wax technique. Length 13 cm. Ferenc Liszt Museum, Sopron.

42 *Mirror-case*. The decorative pattern is coloured black, green and red with sealing-wax and shows a stylized floral motif with its stalk in a heart. Diameter 8.4 cm. Provenance: Transdanubia. Ethnographical Museum, Budapest.

LIST OF COLOUR PLATES

XII *Upper and lower leaf of a mirror-case*, with a flower pattern in sealing-wax inlay that is related to the patterns of frieze-cloak embroidery. 10.3 cm. Provenance: Nemespátró, Somogy County. Rippl-Rónai Museum, Kaposvár.

XIII *Water dipper*, with carved edges and a relief showing a deer and stag. The handle is mounted with a decoration in copper and nickel which imitates the Austrian coat of arms, dated 1898. Length 17 cm. Provenance: Nógrád County. Palóc Museum, Balassagyarmat.

XIV *Razor-case*. One-piece turning lid with a flower pattern in sealing-wax. The date 1835 appears on one side. Length: 24 cm. Provenance: Döbörhegy, Vas County. Savaria Museum, Szombathely.

XV *Razor-case*, inlaid with sealing-wax, the date 1824 appears on its upper part. A turning lid shows a tulip and a monstrance below. Length 20 cm. Savaria Museum, Szombathely.

XVI *Field-guard's ax*, with copper work on its head, showing the date 1846. The handle is later, it is metal-inlaid, with patterns in nails and celluloid inlay. The handle is 119.5 cm long. Provenance: Paszab, Szabolcs-Szatmár County. András Jósa Museum, Nyíregyháza.

1 Antal Kapoli sen., carver-herdsman, Kossuth Prize winner (1867–1957)

2 Lajos Garai, horse-herd of Máta, Hortobágy. 1963

3 Mihály Tóth, carver-herdsman. 1943

4 József Ostoróczki, carver-herdsman of Egercsehi, Heves County. 1951

*5 Carvers' knives. Southern Transdanubia (right and left)
and Nógrád County (centre)*

6 Whip-handles. About 1900 and 1920

7 *Shepherd's crook*

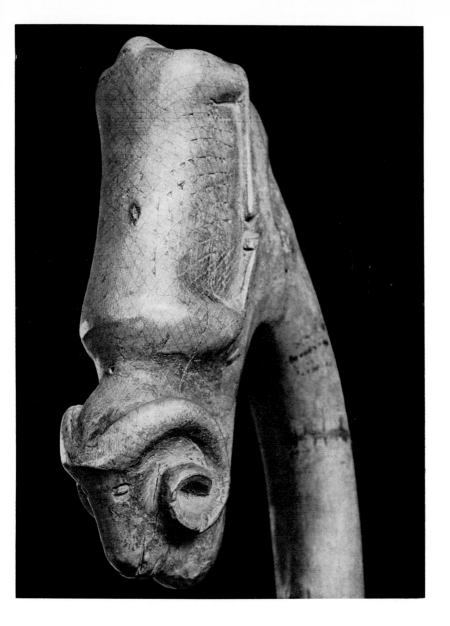

8 Shepherd's crook. Dunaadony-Dajapuszta, Fejér County, turn of the century

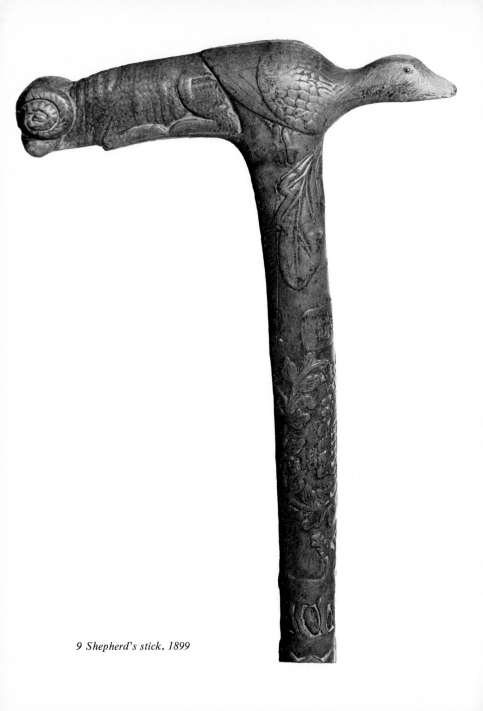

9 Shepherd's stick. 1899

10 Shepherd's crook. Csapod. Győr-Sopron County

11 Shepherd's crook.
Csákvár, Fejér County, 1888

12 Shepherd's crook. Csákberény, Fejér
County, beginning of the 20th century

13 *Razor-case. Bakonybél,*
Veszprém County, 1842

14 *Razor-case. Nagycenk,*
Győr-Sopron County, 1854

15 Shaving-mirror frame

16 Back of a shaving-mirror case. Around 1870

17 Mangling boards with engraved decoration, 1770 (right) and 1829 (left)

18 *Details of the decoration of a mangling board*

19 Swine-herd's ax of Somogy County

*20 Herdsmen's sticks. Szarvas, Békés County (left), Kazár, Nógrád County (centre).
The stick on the right was made in 1860*

21 Cross. Nőtincs, Nógrád
  County, early in the 20th century

22 Cross. Kisterenye, Nógrád County,
  between 1930 and 1940

23 Aspersorium carved of maple-wood

24 *Salt-cellar. Somogy County, 1895*

25 Salt-cellar with scratched decorations

26 Salt-cellar. Buzsák, Somogy County, late in the 1930s

27 Match-box. Buzsák, Somogy County, late in the 1930s

28 Match-box. Szúnyogpuszta, Veszprém County, 1908

◁ *29 Mirror-case. Magyargencs, Vas County, 1840*

◁ *30 Match-box. Szúnyogpuszta, 1909*

31 Bench. Nógrád County, 1910

32 *Watch-chain carved from horn*

33 *Horn, made by Antal Kapoli sen., 1948*

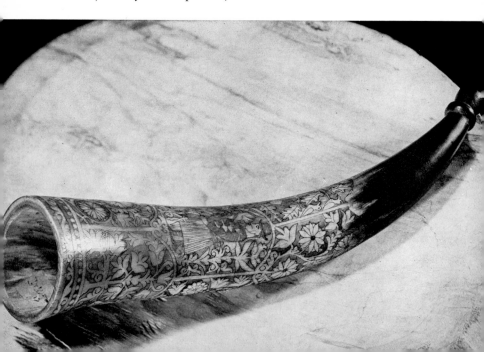

34 Detail of the horn on Plate 33

35 Gourd, made by Antal Kapoli sen.

36 Scab-grease case. Okány, Békés County

37 Water dipper. Nógrád County

38 Water dipper. Heves County, around 1930

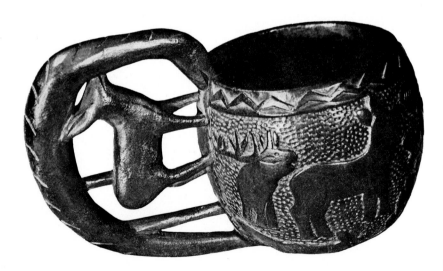

39 Water dipper. Zagyvapálfalva, Nógrád County, 1930

40 Water dipper. Kisterenye, Nógrád County, around 1940

41 Salt and paprika-cellar

42 Mirror-case. Transdanubia